Healing Life's Wounds

Beyond Feeling Broken

Pat Marsh

Copyright © Pat Marsh 2025

First published 2025 by Sarah Grace Publishing,
an imprint of Malcolm Down Publishing Ltd.
www.sarahgracepublishing.co.uk
www.malcolmdown.co.uk

29 28 27 26 25   7 6 5 4 3 2 1

The right of Pat Marsh to be identified as the author of this work has been asserted by her in accordance with the Copyright, Designs and Patents Act 1988.

All rights reserved. No part of this publication may be reproduced, stored in a retrieval system, or transmitted in any other form or by any means, electronic, mechanical, photocopying, recording or otherwise, without the prior permission of the publisher.

British Library Cataloguing in Publication Data
A catalogue record for this book is available from the British Library.

ISBN 978-1-915046-86-4

Unless otherwise indicated, all Scripture quotations are taken from the *Holy Bible*, New Living Translation, copyright © 1996, 2004, 2015 by Tyndale House Foundation. Used by permission of Tyndale House Publishers, Inc., Carol Stream, Illinois 60188. All rights reserved.

Scripture quotations marked MSG are taken from *THE MESSAGE*, copyright © 1993, 2002, 2018 by Eugene H. Peterson. Used by permission of NavPress. All rights reserved. Represented by Tyndale House Publishers, Inc.

Cover design by Esther Kotecha
Art direction by Sarah Grace

Printed in the UK

Endorsements

Healing Life's Wounds is an excellent book. Pat writes from lived experience and she speaks candidly, yet gently, with a deep longing for us to walk with her on the path to healing and peace. Pat has a gift for saying profound things simply. Oh, how our church needs that gift!

The Rt Rev Jan McFarlane, Dean of Lichfield, assistant bishop in the Diocese of Lichfield

It's a rare human life that does not know woundedness. It's a rare author who can turn her own lived experience of betrayal and loss into a practical and sensitive guide to help others move beyond what is trapping them in their pain. Pat is a wounded healer with the vision and the passion to help others find their way to healing.

Margaret Silf, author and retreat leader

Woven throughout with the author's own story, *Healing Life's Wounds* is an honest portrayal of how hope, peace and healing can be found in the bleakest of situations. Gently presented, at a pace that doesn't overwhelm the reader, simple exercises act as helpful stepping stones along the way to healing. There are precious diamonds to be found in this book.

Gilana Young, author and survivor of childhood abuse

What a beautiful book! It's one of the most enlightening books around healing that I have read.

Sheila Jacobs, writer, editor and award-winning author

This simple book is full of profound truths and practical exercises that are not necessarily simple to do but are the root to freedom and release. Reading the book feels like being held in a warm embrace by a sensitive and empathetic friend who is prepared to sit with you among the painful emotions you are experiencing and lead you deeper into the loving and safe arms of Jesus. The exercises are clear and helpful without being prescriptive and build chapter by chapter to help the reader face their wounds without fear. Pat achieves a wonderful balance of encouraging the responsibility each of us needs to take to do our own work, with the need to trust and rely on Jesus for the strength and love to do this work. A really helpful, beautiful and practical book for anyone wanting to move into more freedom and lightness.

Catriona Futter, Christian life coach

Healing Life's Wounds is packed with helpful advice and useful information for those who are dwelling in a dark place and in need of healing, but it is far from being merely a 'self-help manual'. Written by one who has suffered from emotional trauma, but who has emerged, not only healed, but at peace and stronger for the experience, Pat takes her readers gently by the hand and leads them to a place of peace and radical healing. There, through prayer, they are able to connect with a God who is *love* and who loves unconditionally.

Pat writes, 'I am now convinced that all our healing is brought about by the most transforming, radical love that you will ever encounter in your life: God's love.' Through the pages of this remarkable book, you too can experience that love and find the peace and healing that our loving heavenly Father is longing to bring you.

Geraldine Elliot-Smith, retired GP and elder of the Order of Jacob's Well

In this very readable book, Pat gives us permission to be honest about our lives by sharing her own painful story. In doing this she pours out hope upon us, and by suggesting a variety of practical approaches to engage with our pain, we are encouraged to open the door to God's goodness to allow his stream of healing to flow.

Rev John Ryeland, former director of the Christian Healing Mission

This book was exactly what I needed! The gentle yet firm words, ideas and reflections were very helpful and were tied into the author's own experiences in ways that meant I experienced empathy without judgement, and sympathy without overload. And as a spiritual counsellor, I found the book full of useful ways to help others going through tough times, with some of the reflections and meditations being great to work through with clients.

Rev Penelope Swithinbank, author and spiritual counsellor

If you are seeking help with emotional pain, *Healing Life's Wounds* is a good place to begin the journey to recovery. Pat does not pretend that this will be an easy path, or that you may not need specialist help as well, but she does offer the hope – based on hard-won personal experience – of significant healing and freedom. Built around insights from her own painful story, and with practical exercises to help apply those truths to our own situation, this book offers hope that change is possible, especially as we seek God's help. It will take time, but Pat is a reliable and sensitive guide, and can be trusted.

Tony Horsfall, author, mentor and retreat leader
Jilly Horsfall, counsellor and retreat leader

Are you seeking a way through pain or turmoil? Providing affirmation, space, peace and gentle challenge, Pat Marsh is a sensitive guide and an authentic companion on the journey.

Emily Owen, author, educator and inspirational speaker

Can I really find relief from this pain? Yes, says Pat Marsh resoundingly. She leads us through a gentle but deep exploration of what lies beneath the anguish as she points us to the One who sets us free. She's a trustworthy guide who understands what we're feeling, having trodden the road of suffering before finding freedom and release in God. I'll recommend this book in the years to come.

Amy Boucher Pye, author and spiritual director

If you want a friend who understands deep hurt and pain yet offers hope, this book is for you. I already have a list of friends to give it to!

Susan Alexander Yates, speaker, blogger and author

Pat Marsh's book, *Healing Life's Wounds*, has grown out of her years of leading healing retreats, and also her personal healing journey. It is a must-read for anyone who is ready to go on their own healing journey and is looking for practical tools to help them with their inner healing. The 'Pause Points' within the book provide the reader with a valuable resource which, if implemented, will be of continuing help throughout life.

Vicki Cottingham, author and retreat leader

An inspiring and comforting narrative as we are invited to get in touch with and face our deep inner feelings, pain and emotions and embrace silence and forgiveness as an essential path to healing.

Edwina Gateley, poet, author and public speaker

Contents

A Note from the Author	11
Introduction	13
Getting the Most from This Book	17
Chapter 1: Feeling Broken	19
Chapter 2: Getting Started	31
Chapter 3: Those Strange Sensations	45
Chapter 4: Defusing Your Emotions	55
Chapter 5: The Inner Story	69
Chapter 6: New Perspectives	81
Chapter 7: The Question of Forgiveness	93
Chapter 8: Letting Go	107
Chapter 9: Actively Forgiving	117
Chapter 10: The Problem of Worry	129
Chapter 11: The Power of the Pause	139
Chapter 12: One Step at a Time	151
Finally . . .	159
Postscript: Words of Encouragement	161
Appendix 1: Helpful Resources on Prayer	163

Appendix 2: Further Healing Resources Written by Pat Marsh	167
Appendix 3: Sources of Help in an Emergency	169
About the Author	171
Acknowledgements	173
End Notes	177

A Note from the Author

This book is not a substitute for professional help and support from qualified healthcare professionals, but rather an additional resource to give you insights, and a shoulder to lean on, as you journey through your painful emotions. It does not offer a complete solution to complex mental issues, nor is it medically exclusive. It is, however, a distillation of my own experiences in finding peace from pain and in guiding others to such a place through twenty years of leading healing retreats. Talking therapies, especially, and other forms of medical help may be an important part of your healing process and I recommend that you consider finding additional help of that nature if need be.

Introduction

So, you are hurting? Hurting very badly? Maybe life has gone pear-shaped, and you have woken up trapped in a deep, dark well of pain, with no sign of a ladder to climb your way out. You are stuck in a vortex of difficult emotions. You hate how you feel.

If any of that feels familiar, this book is for you. This is a lifeline for you to grab on to. Catch hold of it, hang on tight and let the lessons in this book help you haul your way out. You might gather the odd scratch along the way. Sometimes you might slip back a bit. But you'll get there.

The clue is in the title: *Healing Life's Wounds*. Sometimes you just cannot see how to. In fact, you doubt if you ever can. You fear that life will never be the same again, and you seriously don't like it. You don't like it one bit. It all feels so desperately hopeless, as if all the odds are stacked against you. You simply don't have the energy or the resources to find your way through.

Ring any bells with you?

If so, this book is written for you; written by someone who has been to those awful dark places of the mind and who has successfully and happily emerged on the other side. It is a book that acknowledges the sometimes messy, always imperfect and often painful reality of the complexity of human experience. It looks at pain and anguish, anger and tears, fear and turmoil, and whatever other gut-wrenching emotions you might be shouldering today. Nothing is off limits. This is a book about the whole, complex, messy lot of it.

It will help you out of that dark and painful place, easing you out using understanding, compassion, practical help and prayer. I write from a Christian perspective because I can do no other; a follower of Jesus is who I now am. God met me in the depths of my brokenness and that began to change everything. Essentially a practical book, however, this is not exclusively about prayer as the only source of healing. But the value of prayer, and an encouragement to explore it, is woven throughout the practical exercises, lived experiences and psychological insights you will find within these pages.

We will explore how your incredible body is always trying to heal itself, and how you can help it to do just that. Many of the weird feelings you may be experiencing are simply messages from your body, often resulting from unprocessed emotions. This book will teach you how to release those emotions safely so that any strange sensations will hopefully begin to calm down. We will also explore how the cycle of your suffering is being perpetuated by the stories you are telling yourself.

We will have to go to a few places you might not want to go to. But it will be for your own good. We'll discuss a couple of things you probably feel you don't want to know about, but they are things which will help you massively: forgiveness and acceptance. And we'll explore how to underpin and help your recovery through praying your way through every step. Encountering Jesus through prayer and stillness was integral to my own healing journey and subsequently transformed my life. This book will mirror that journey, step by simple step.

I am now convinced that all our healing is brought about by the most transforming, radical love that you will ever encounter in your life: God's love. But I totally get that God can sometimes feel devastatingly absent when you need him most, so you wonder if all you have ever heard about him can possibly be true. These pages will gently guide you through your doubts.

Ultimately, this is a book about hope; about finding hope in situations where there appears to be no hope, and about finding glimmers of light in what might be an all-consuming darkness. It can help you to find peace and to lead a happier, richer, fuller life than you might currently think possible. My desire is that it will be for you a stepping-stone on the journey towards healing. But you must take your courage in your hands, stretch out your leg and take the first step, trusting that the raging waters of your struggles won't swamp you and that there really is an invisible Someone holding your hand.

So come; join me on the journey, knowing that I write not as one who has my own life perfectly sorted out, or as a person who never feels difficult emotions, but as a fellow traveller on the way to wholeness and happiness. I have struggled through some deep, dark, depressing places. I have lived through loss, breakdown, betrayal and grief, and a whole host of other things I wish I had never had to face. But I have learned how to emerge into a place of peace and happiness, no matter what life throws at me.

Get ready to catch the lifeline. Here it comes…

Pat Marsh

Getting the Most from This Book

There are as many ways to read a book as there are readers. Some will habitually look at the ending first, while others browse the chapter headings and dive headlong into the one that seems to resonate most. Some people will pick out the suggested exercises and simply work with those, while others will skip them completely. Avid readers will quickly skim read the whole text, racing through it at pace. And some people will patiently work slowly through the book, letting each new chapter fully sink in before progressing.

The latter is what I suggest. Each chapter builds on the teaching of the previous one, so I recommend that you *work through the book sequentially*. It is also worth taking your time with the text, letting each bit of writing connect with your own experience and drawing out from it what feels helpful to you. Don't be tempted to rush; work through it *at the pace that is right for you.*

Don't skip the 'Pause Points': they are important in helping you learn to connect with yourself in moments of stillness, in helping you to reflect, and in guiding you, as you progress through them, to a deeper understanding of how to work towards freedom from your debilitating emotions.

Even if writing is not normally your thing, I recommend you read with *a notebook* by your side. Use it to jot down key insights, to journal through some of the questions the book poses, and to generally 'get all the thoughts out of your head'. Writing is both cathartic and an important aid to remembering.

Healing is deep work. And sometimes hard work. But always, always worth the effort. Be aware, though, that all manner of memories may be stirred as you work through the book, so you might find it helpful to have *someone to talk things through with*. Perhaps a friend, a therapist, a pastor or someone similar might be willing to be a trusted, confidential listener for you.

Let's get started.

CHAPTER 1

Feeling Broken

When we have the courage to walk
into our story and own it,
we get to write the ending.
Brené Brown[1]

The future begins today.
Wayne Gerard Trotman[2]

The broken tree

Sitting outdoors one day, I noticed a tree. It stood out like a scar on the landscape. The view before me was one of beautiful, quintessentially English, summer countryside. Gently rolling landscape, vibrantly alive bushes and trees, fields bright with ripening corn, swallows swooping and diving under a cloudless blue sky, and right in the middle, centre stage, the disfigured skeleton of what remained of a broken tree. It held my attention. I wondered how it came to be so broken amid such flourishing aliveness.

Brokenness is not the natural order of things. But sometimes it happens. Maybe a lightning strike was what had crippled that tree. Perhaps a slow, lingering condition had taken it. Possibly it was planted in the wrong place. Or maybe its roots had been irreparably damaged? Who knows? But there it was, right in the middle of this otherwise beautiful scene: a skeletal, broken tree, its natural vitality and aliveness crippled by some unknown circumstance.

Sometimes we can feel like that tree; the rest of the world apparently flourishing around us while we are still there in the landscape of our life but feeling utterly broken inside. Lots of things can bring us to that place. We may have experienced the 'lightning strike' of a tragic and devastating accident, or the sudden and unexpected loss of someone dear to us. Maybe our current feelings are the result of a slow building unhappiness that has established itself over time to the point of now being unbearable; a lingering and increasingly painful 'dis-ease' with our life. Or possibly we too have 'damaged our roots'; allowed ourselves, for whatever reason, to stop living out of our own deeply held values.

Many things can take us to that broken place. It happens. Lots of us carry hidden wounds that are silently weeping within us. Unaddressed, those quietly weeping wounds can often build into a pent-up insistent scream, an inner megaphone that we can no longer ignore, and that scream can lead us to pick up a book like this.

A landscape photographer might well have photoshopped that broken tree out of his image. Alas, we cannot do that in our own lives. Our remarkable brains and bodies retain the memories of all we have experienced. Everything. Both joyous and painful. As Jo Saxton writes, 'The people around us have left their mark . And personal experiences don't remain in the past. They leave a deep imprint, forever changing us.'[3] No matter how much we might want to do so, we cannot selectively erase some of the things that have happened to us or words that have been spoken over us. They leave their imprint.

We all have broken pieces in our lives. None of us have had a perfect past (whatever we think that might look like). We cannot photoshop out the experiences that have wounded us, or the behaviours we wish we had never adopted. That is the heart and soul of this book. We are all wounded. But all can heal. As therapist Simon Parke says, 'Our past can throw strong shadows across our path, but it need not define us.'[4]

Life is not always easy. It doesn't always go smoothly. Sometimes the things we've experienced have wounded us enormously and caused us deep emotional pain. Even the people who mean most to us can hurt us sometimes by the words they speak or the things they do or don't do. We often can, unintentionally, do the same to them. Because none of us are perfect. Every single one of us is a 'work in progress'. We are all just doing the best that we are capable of at the time.

Scuffs and scratches

One day, many years ago, my son was doing the best he was capable of, as he careered around the lawn on his little red tractor. At three years old he hadn't quite mastered the intricacies of steering. Undeterred, he raced on. With each new circuit his shiny toy accumulated increasing signs of wear and tear as he scraped the gatepost, bumped into the wall, mounted the rockery and generally drove more in the manner of an enthusiastic rally driver than a cautious farmer. The scratches and scuff marks he gathered along the way became the tell-tale signs of a little boy at play.

Unlike my young son's tractor, we can't always see the scuff marks on humans, at least not directly. A lot of us carry them inside ourselves. We internalise them. They reside in our memory cells. For many different reasons, we choose not to show them directly to the world. We lock them away and keep them safely buried inside ourselves, usually because we are afraid that people will like us less if we wear them on the outside. This can seem like a good idea at the time, but in the long run it takes its toll.

When we don't attend to our scuffs and scratches, if life becomes even more difficult, the wounds we carry become more and more of a burden, until there comes a day when we realise that we simply can't shoulder them any longer. They develop into a heavy unhappiness, maybe even a serious depression, that limits our lives, colours all our reactions and becomes unbearable.
A dark cloud descends over our mind, uncomfortable emotions and painful thoughts dominate our inner world and, in the worst-case scenario, there seems no way out.

But the good news is that with the right help and support, there is always a way out.

Change only happens when it is more painful to stay as we are than to engage with the work involved in changing. We may have been unhappy for a long time, but successfully and skilfully avoided putting our true feelings under the microscope. But when we finally hit rock bottom, that is the place where there's nowhere else to run to. Brokenness can take us to that place; the place where the inner pain of our wounds has grown too loud for us to ignore any longer. It can be a frightening place, but it is the threshold of a healing space. It is also the place where God can meet us in our vulnerability, as he did with me.

Through the door

It was never going to be easy, to dig myself out of the big black hole of my emotions. At times, it seemed an impossible task, as if the darkness of months was all enveloping and never-ending. It was never going to be easy. But I knew I had to try. Somehow, I had to find a way to rediscover that elusive thing called peace.

That's what led me to be standing at the heavy, carved wooden door. I paused, took my courage in both hands, and reached up towards the bell. Finally, with absolutely no idea of what I might find on the other side of the imposing threshold, I pressed the button. An immediate loud and excited barking, which must surely have been coming from the voice box of an exceptionally large and threatening dog, was certainly not the response I had expected. When the door finally creaked open, a small lady with a welcoming smile stood before me with, at her feet, a pint-sized little terrier. I had arrived. And I was welcome.

That was where an amazing story began. A story of transformation that continues to evolve to this day. A story that has changed me; one of healing and new life.

What I discovered on the other side of that door was Love; love with a capital 'L'. I had gone there in search of solitude. What I found, to my amazement, was that I was, in truth, far from alone. I had neither expected nor sought the experience, but I found myself enfolded in a depth of presence which I was only later able to name as 'God'. I was surrounded and strengthened by tangible love; a love that manifested itself as a depth of feeling that I couldn't begin to describe. I couldn't understand it, didn't comprehend it, but its impact was profound. It felt like a heaven-touching-earth moment.

That was the start of an exciting, often confusing, journey. I knew nothing of God at that point, had never read a Bible and only went to church for weddings and funerals. But I knew, in one of those indescribable moments when you just 'know that you know', that I had met God in that place, or rather, that he had chosen to meet with me. In my brokenness, God had broken through.

The short version of the story of the years which followed is that, over time, I climbed out of that deep, dark hole and found a happier, more contented life. I delved deeply into what the 'God story' was all about, began to pray more, worked hard at my healing, and emerged into a whole new way of living. I gave up my career and stepped into a role which led me ultimately to helping others to find healing. It has been the greatest privilege and the most rewarding work of my life.

We all live out our different stories as we travel through this world. My story didn't begin there. That doorstep was just a transition point between before and after, between the past and what was still to come. It took significant courage to face my story and accept it; to own it so that I could, as Brené Brown says, write a new ending.[5]

So, I wonder what your unique story is? What is the story that has led you inside the covers of this book? It may be that you are in a very painful place, as I once was. It may be that your life, as you expected it to be, has been completely shattered, and that you feel in a deep, dark impossible-to-get-out-of hole. Or it might be that you have a rumbling discomfort about how things are, and you are not exactly sure what you are seeking but you just know 'there must be more to life than this'. Possibly you can't quite articulate your thinking beyond saying that you know you are searching for something, anything, that will help. It may be that you are simply curious. Whoever you are, and however you find yourself today, you are welcome here. In these pages you can find the beginnings of hope and healing. You can walk into a new, and better, story; as I did when I stepped, like the children in Narnia,[6] through that retreat house door.

Everyone has their own unique story. There never has been and there never will be another you. As Marléne Rose Shaw puts it, 'Even though there are seven billion of us on our beautiful planet Earth, each of us is unique. Our stories are the dreams we dream and the adventures we have. They are our disappointments and our successes and all that happens in between.'[7]

Our stories include our failures and our losses, our wounds and our scars, and all those things we wish had not been part of our experience. For each one of us, those things will be different. But, make no mistake about it, we are all wounded in some way. It happens to us all. Life is like that. But that doesn't mean that those wounds need to dominate our lives. If we are open to the possibility, there are ways to find healing of our inner wounds, and with that healing we can then begin to live a richer, fuller, more content and fruitful life.

Since my own experience with a deep, dark, black hole of emotion and pain – the one that led me to step through that door – I have become passionate about helping others to find their inner healing. I have been hugely blessed, over time, to find a place of deep healing, and it is my heartfelt desire that others should experience the same. Because we only get one shot at this life, and it is the greatest shame to waste any more time than necessary in angst and pain.

Does that mean we will never experience times of unhappiness and inner turmoil? No, of course not. But learning how to face those moments head-on, and with whom, can be life-transforming. Does my experience mean that there are no other ways to find peace? Possibly not. But if my story helps to improve your story, every step of my journey and every word in this book will have been worth it.

Life is tough. Things go wrong. Circumstances don't always work out as we hoped. Dreams get dashed. People get hurt. We make mistakes. To be human is to experience the whole spectrum of emotions. Our inner world is not always peaceful. There are times when difficult thoughts rumble around in there and refuse to be silenced. Worries about the future. Regrets about the past. Fears for our wellbeing. Grief for our losses. The pain of our wounds. Anger about the way we have been treated. Deep and complex hurts about our life situation. It can become overwhelming. If that is how it is for you today, please know that you will find a compassionate presence within these pages.

It's OK to not be OK

Several mental health organisations are now using that phrase as a strapline, and it is a message we all need to take to heart. As Patrick Regan, an advocate for good mental health, writes, 'it's OK not to be OK'.[8] It's perfectly OK. There is nothing inherently wrong with you if you are not feeling bright and chirpy. It is part of human nature. Somehow, we have grown up absorbing the message of our culture that it is a sign of weakness to admit that we are not feeling OK. But it isn't. If anything, being willing to be vulnerably open about your mental struggles is a sign of strength. It can be the first step towards healing. No one person has it all together all the time, even if we might imagine that they do.

There are, of course, varying degrees of mental struggles. Sometimes difficult thoughts and emotions become so dominant that they are all-consuming, and it is practically impossible to see beyond them. They can so cloud our mind that we can't think clearly about anything else. Even the smallest tasks of everyday living can feel like we have a mountain to climb. It can feel as if we are drifting around in a fog of pain; existing in the world but totally disconnected from it. We find ourselves ruminating continuously on our unhappiness, on our desire and our longing for things to be different. We find ourselves in a very dark and broken place.

All kinds of things might have led us to that place. We might have experienced some significant trauma or a series of hurts and difficulties which have built up over a prolonged period. We all have a different path to that broken place. But most of us arrive there at least once in our lives. If even a small amount of that strikes a chord with you, please read on. If your symptoms are less severe, this book is still for you.

There is hope. Healing is possible.

Standing on shaky ground

When we're feeling fragile, we can feel as if we are permanently standing on shaky ground. We may well even be able to feel that shakiness in our body. The circumstances that have led us to that place have rocked our confidence in others, in the inherent goodness of the world and especially in ourselves. Nothing feels secure anymore. It can feel as if the world as we knew it, or as we always thought it would be, has forever changed. And we have yet to find a way to live confidently into the new.

As you try to find a way forward, you need to be constantly mindful of how much energy you have in the tank each day. You need to care for yourself along the way. If you are in an exhausted emotional place, where the smallest everyday tasks of life feel beyond you, you need to take heed of these wise words from Patrick Regan's book, *Honesty Over Silence*: 'The plan is this: you do what you can, when you can, however you can, with whatever you've got. And if you can't, you can't. You rest until you can again.'[9]

CHAPTER 2

Getting Started

Almost everything will work again if you unplug it for a few minutes, including you.
Anne Lamott[10]

Be still, and know that I am God!
Psalm 46:10

The keys to healing

When I was in my own deep, dark hole of pain, God was some vaguely distant entity, until one day he suddenly wasn't. Since that encounter, I have felt particularly drawn to study Jesus' ministry of healing, of which there are many accounts in the Bible. The thing about Jesus is that he both taught and modelled the way to live. He didn't just give us what appears to be a list of rules and regulations for getting into heaven; he gave profoundly good advice about how to live healthily, free of deep inner pain. This book will explore why our minds and bodies feel as they do and will look at some very practical actions to help you ease the uncomfortable sensations and overcome any mental turmoil. But really, Jesus says it all. And he says it so simply:

> Don't worry. Don't be afraid.
> Don't be angry. Forgive often.
> Let go of your burdens. Be thankful.
> Be still. Rest. Pray. [11]

Sounds easy. Except that it's not. That's a challenging list if you're feeling angry or afraid, churned up, bitter, or resentful. And it might be incredibly hard to think of anything to be thankful for today. Those words can feel as if they are piling on more pressure at a time when you're struggling to simply keep your head above water. In fact, if you're feeling depressed and overwhelmed, those things can feel utterly impossible. But they're not. They really are not. They are not achieved overnight but they are possible, at least to some degree. Those simple statements, which I've paraphrased above, are important keys to health. And we are going to explore them in very practical ways.

Do you want to get well?

Firstly, though, never forget that you alone can make the choice to make this healing journey. No one else is responsible for your wellbeing. Only you. It can be tempting to blame others for where you are at emotionally, and that may be partly true. It is entirely natural and very easy to fall into the trap of blaming other people. Not just blaming them but falsely thinking that we can never get well again unless *they* change. All our negative thoughts about them keep us stuck in a cycle of blame, which makes us unwell and deflects us away from the possibility of ever changing our situation and our feelings. We erroneously think that the only solution to our pain is for the *other person* to change. But we cannot make that happen. We can, however, take responsibility for our own thoughts and actions.

In the Bible there is a story about a man lying by a pool[12] and another about a beggar sitting at the roadside.[13] The man lying by the pool was unable to walk and the beggar was blind, and Jesus healed them both. But he didn't restore them immediately. In each case, he first asked a question. To the man lying by the pool he said, 'Would you like to get well?'[14] To the blind man he said, 'What do you want me to do for you?'[15] Under the circumstances, these were both questions to which the answers seemed obvious, but Jesus asked them, nevertheless. Apparently, God wants us to want to heal. God seems to want us to be proactive.

Making the choice

Whatever has led you to this point in your life, you have a choice. As clinical social worker Victoria Priya writes, 'You may not have had power over what happened to you in the past, but you have complete power about how you respond and how you move forward, starting today.'[16] You can and must make the choice to take the responsibility for your wellbeing into your own hands, regardless of your external circumstances. You need to drop the blame game. Life is not perfect. Things often work out differently to how you hoped they would. And that can create enormous pain. But that doesn't mean that you can't move on and find peace and health and a new enthusiasm for life. Because you can. But it starts with that choice: to do what *you* need to do to get well.

This book will guide you through some important, helpful and healing processes which you can work through largely unaided. But first, you must make the choice to take your future wellbeing into your own hands. You have the power to make that choice, regardless of what anyone else in your life thinks, says or does.

Finding support

Never underestimate how helpful it can be to share your story with a wise and compassionate person. Someone outside the current circle of your problems. Someone who can allow you to speak out the tangled turmoil of your thoughts.

Difficult though it is, it is important to recognise that you might need such help. It can be hard to make the healing journey alone. We all need support. It takes courage to ask for that support, but it may be what you need to do, and there is no shame in that. I have known what it is like to struggle to take my mask off and 'be real' with people. Honesty is always the first tentative step towards healing. Brené Brown, an expert on vulnerability, says 'When we deny our stories, they define us. When we own our stories, we get to write a brave new ending.'[17]

We find it easy to make conversation about things which are outside our control, like what the chance of rain is today, but generally much harder to share the difficult issues we may be carrying in our hearts. But being open about such things with the right person is vitally important. Simply talking about your pain, sharing all that is troubling you, can be helpful in untangling the threads of your story, loosening the knots in your mind, especially if you share your thoughts with a wise listener. Speaking it out also helps to create some much-needed space in your head. It stops the incessant inner conversations that are only heading in a negative direction. It gives your brain some temporary respite. So, take some time to carefully reflect on who you might honestly share your feelings with. Who might be a helpful listener for you? Take your courage in your hands and arrange to meet them. Talking to the right person always helps. Our healing is never complete until we have been fully heard.

And of course, you can turn to Jesus in prayer; the Jesus who promised, 'I am with you always'.[18] He will always be there for you, no matter how messy your life might seem, and his love knows no limits. Jesus invites you to bring your burdens to him and he promises he will 'give you rest' from them.[19]

Resting the mind

Any form of suffering has both a physical and a mental component. No matter what the balance is between what you are experiencing in your mind and in your body, calming your inner world will make an important contribution to your wellbeing. This is true even if your greatest problem is chronic physical pain, as being anxious or upset about your condition will only make it feel worse.

Whatever you are going through, you will rarely be able to make wise decisions or see a way forward if your mind is in turmoil; finding some respite from any emotional pain which has you in its grip is an important first step, because suffering can often be exhausting on a day-to-day, moment-by-moment basis. If you can carve out pockets of time where you can distance yourself from the environment in which you feel at your worst, it is important to do so. Put yourself in a different place for a little while. If home is where the darkness feels heaviest, get out of the house from time to time. If it is work, get out of the workplace for a bit. If it is being with certain people, find a way to distance yourself from them for a short period of time. Give yourself space; space where you can temporarily escape the worst of the stresses. Space where you can let the tensions out, exhale, breathe. Space where you can cry if you need to. Time in nature will be especially helpful if you can manage it. A woodland walk. The local park. A few moments in a garden. Green space is very healing.

Our minds are rarely quiet. From waking to sleeping, our heads keep up a constant inner chatter. Revisiting the past. Thinking about the future. Endlessly cycling through our problems. Worrying about things which may never happen. Wishing we could rewind our life and live it differently. Our minds never stop. Stillness and silence may be the last thing we seek out when we are feeling broken. But both are marvellously good for us, and they rest our endlessly churning brain. There are many sound medical reasons for incorporating silence into our days. Calmness and stillness boost the immune system, reduce inflammation, help prevent disease and slow ageing.[20]

Learning how to become still really is a win-win situation.

This is especially important when we are feeling fragile. We all need relaxation. For some, that will mean getting out in the fresh air, participating in exercise. Others will choose to curl up with a good book or take a long leisurely soak in the bath. Some will choose to socialise over a pint or simply take a nap. For others, it will be baking bread, listening to music, or getting out in the garden. Everyone has their own preferred way of relaxing. But how often do you really switch off totally? Fully, completely, totally? For many of us, the answer is almost never.

Cultivating stillness

All inner healing needs deep, slow, unhurried moments of stillness and quiet. In fact, I suspect there can be no true inner healing without this kind of reflective time. We all need moments when we totally switch off from the demands of the world, and more so when we are troubled. I don't mean flopping in front of the television set or idly scrolling through your social media feed. Those things may enable you to temporarily zone out, but they will also give your brain more stimulation to process. What I'm talking about is silence. Pure, uninterrupted silence. Even if we only experience it in the briefest of moments, it makes a difference to our mind, body and physiology. It can relax us fully and we need that.

You may resist being face to face with your pain, with all your familiar distractions stripped away. In our noise-saturated world, you may well think that you can't cope with silence. But you can. Think of your troubled thoughts as being like waves on a stormy sea. Even on the most violent ocean, if you were able to sink just 10ft below the waves you would find, at that depth, that the sea is perfectly still. It is just the same with your mind. It is possible to sink into silence, no matter how turbulent your thoughts are. It may take a little practise. But it's possible. You simply need to begin, a little at a time. Why not try it now?

Pause Point

The Stillness Spot

Sit in a quiet peaceful spot; somewhere where you won't be disturbed. Sit in a way that is comfortable but upright, with your feet on the ground in front of you and your hands gently relaxed on your lap. It will help if you can close your eyes after you have read these instructions.

Now breathe. Become aware of your breathing. Breathe in through your nose, letting your breathing be relaxed and slow, but not forced. Notice the cool air entering your nostrils and feel your chest expanding as your lungs fill. Hold that breath for a moment, slightly longer than normal. Then let it go. Breathe it out. As you exhale, notice your chest returning to normal and notice warm air flowing out through your nose.

Do this a few times, slowly and deliberately, and then let your breathing settle into its natural, steady rhythm. With each in and out breath concentrate on all the sensations of the air entering and leaving your body. Really notice what is happening as your body does this most natural of things: breathing.

Whenever your mind gets distracted, just return to focus on your breath.

Pray, in whatever way feels right for you.

When it feels like a good time to stop, gently open your eyes, and return to where you are.

Notice if you are feeling any different now.

Sinking below the noise

This most simple of practices can really help you to become still, both inwardly and outwardly, no matter how wound up your mind is, or how frenetic your day. Taking several slow, deep breaths also releases any stress from your body and helps to calm you. It may feel a little unnatural at first but as you keep returning to this it will become easier, and you will begin to appreciate the benefits of taking small moments of stillness in the busyness of your days. Even just five or ten minutes will help. The more you do it, the more you will find that your mind becomes a little clearer, a little less stressed. It will help to rest your brain and slowly untangle the knots of your troubled thoughts, and that is important for beginning to heal.

But I wonder what you felt as you did that simple exercise? Strange? Rested? Self-conscious? Peaceful? Or maybe quite conflicted? Was there a little voice in your head questioning why you were doing this? If being intentionally silent is a new experience for you, then it is more than likely that you may have felt all those things and more. It is also quite likely that the thoughts you were 'trying not to think' became annoyingly louder in that time. As Charles Ringma writes, it's completely normal for our restless senses to catapult us from one thing to another.[21] I like to think of it as my thoughts being like buses driving past in my mind. I can notice the bus but that doesn't mean I have to jump on it. I can simply let it go past. Everyone finds their mind wandering when they attempt to be still, especially when they are new to the practice. That is why it's good to try to really focus on your breathing, which is always with you, wherever you are, and which gives your mind a different focus.

Now here is the radical bit. Though you might not name it as such, silence is a form of prayer. By being deeply silent you are not only giving your brain some respite from the struggle; you are also prayerfully opening yourself up to the presence of God, who is always longing to connect with you. Learning to do this is a first step towards healing. Frank Skinner, in *A Comedian's Prayer Book*, speaks of it like this: 'It isn't not-praying. It feels more like being prayed.'[22]

Looking with awareness

Just looking with awareness at the natural environment is another practice that can lead us into a stillness below our troubled thoughts. When we are truly looking at something with all our focus, when we are observing it deeply, our otherwise ruminating thoughts fade into the background. If you are unaccustomed to silence, this exercise may feel easier than the previous one.

As you read this, you, like me, are sitting on a ball of rock that is spinning at 740km per second, while at the same time travelling round the sun at the speed of 30km per second, and we don't even feel as if we are moving. How amazing is that? As the Bible puts it, we live in a 'wildly wonderful world'.[23] Furthermore, while you are careering through the universe, 5 litres of blood are being pumped every forty-five seconds through the 100,000km of blood vessels in your body, and your brain is interpreting the patterns of ink on this paper into images and words that make sense to you. So much more is also going on inside you and around you, without you making any of it happen. Each one of us, as we read in the Psalms, is 'fearfully and wonderfully made'.[24] We truly are each a miracle of biological engineering, living within an amazing world.

Take a pause now to gaze at that 'wildly wonderful world' and let it still your churning thoughts.

Pause Point

Simple gazing

Sit by an open window or stand outside in the fresh air for a moment.

Put this book down and simply look. Gaze at everything around you without attaching any story to it.

Just look. Soak up the wonder and the miracle of the flowers, the trees, the architecture, the ants on the path; whatever it is that you can see.

Allow your eyes to land on something and simply enjoy it in all its detail. Just look.

And just feel. Notice the sensation of the breeze, or the warmth of the sunshine, or the feel of raindrops on your face; whatever the weather is offering you today. Hear the sounds around you. Take a deep breath and taste the air.

Do nothing. Just look. Just feel. Just be.

Be aware of the wonder of this quite remarkable world and voice some prayers of thanks.

When you are ready, settle down and pick up this book again.

A journal for the journey

The exercises and notes woven throughout this book are integral to helping you to move forward. Some of them will challenge you, others may surprise you and many may give you critical insights. Writing things down is an important way of consolidating things in your mind. I mentioned this earlier. If you haven't already done so, get a simple notebook and use it to jot down regularly all the points you want to remember. Make it a positive tool in your recovery. Put it on your shopping list now!

CHAPTER 3

Those Strange Sensations

Fear arises in our enslaving imaginations.
Simon Parke[25]

Do not be afraid, for I am with you.
Isaiah 43:5

The shattering

Let's look now at some of those turbulent feelings.

The family heirloom lay in broken bits on the kitchen floor. Shattered into countless fragments. In a careless moment I had let the precious vase, the one that had been handed down through four generations, slip through my fingers. There it was. Broken. Never to be the same again. No matter that I had never really liked it. Or that it would not have been my choice of ornament. The fact was that I had history with it. It had always been part of my family life in one way or another and I thought it always would be. But now it lay in pieces. Shattered.

Sometimes life gets shattered like that. In a single unpredictable instant, we are hit with the reality that life as we knew it will never be the same again. Maybe it was like that for you. Maybe something happened on one moment of one day which changed everything for you; a moment in time that will be forever imprinted on your memory. Or perhaps your struggles intensified over time. Sometimes the trajectory of our hopes and longings unravels slowly, until we reach the point of knowing that things are no longer working, that we don't want to live like this anymore. Sometimes, in the very worst-case scenario, we feel as if we no longer want to live, full stop. Sometimes, like my family heirloom, we have held on to things for a long time until there comes a day when we realise that it is all slipping through our fingers; we can hold it together no longer.

When the pieces of our life get shattered, when we cannot see a way to put them back together, it can be scary. Superglue is a wonderful invention but even that can't mend everything that breaks. But there is help. There will be a way through.

When we are in a broken place, any stability we previously enjoyed feels horribly shattered. The hopes and dreams we had for life may be lying in pieces and we cannot initially see how on earth we are going to put those pieces back together again. Possibly the broken bits will never fit back together in quite the same way. Life is going to be different from now on. Or maybe we are in a situation where we know life could be better, if only we could see how to make it so.

All this has a hugely disorientating impact on our wellbeing, both mentally and physically. It is never just the distress in our heads that gets us down. We can feel so dreadfully unwell too. A racing heart, headache, nausea, shakiness, a tight chest, dreadful fatigue; we may feel all those sensations and more. We wonder what on earth is happening to us. We simply don't feel ourselves anymore, and there is so much going on with our crippling thoughts that the physical sensations compound our distress.

The physiology of fear

Beyond the unique life experiences that led you to this point, there are reasons for the strange sensations you feel in your body. The body, mind, and spirit are all designed to operate together as an integrated whole. And that is both part of the problem and part of the solution. We often have the capacity to keep on keeping on through quite horrendous circumstances before we allow ourselves to properly stop and work out how to address the situation. Our physiology is so powerfully linked to our emotions that our bodies are often screaming at us that something is wrong, long before we come to a point where we give ourselves permission to face up to that fact.

Much of this arises through the body's inbuilt mechanisms which are designed to keep us safe in the world. We possess an amazing threat-alert system which kicks into action whenever we have any level of fear, no matter how minor. Our body senses, often before we can articulate it, that something is challenging us deeply, and a protective biological response gets automatically activated. Whether or not we want it to, our body prepares itself to respond to danger. Hence the very strange physical feelings that accompany the emotion of fear. Our heart rate speeds up to pump more blood to our muscles and brain. We breathe faster, as our lungs work to deliver us more oxygen. Our digestive system slows, so that our brain can focus on more immediate things. The pupils of our eyes widen so that we can see better. And all of this happens instantly.

We have a biological response to our fear, and it makes us feel very uncomfortable. But our body is simply trying to protect us. This process is an entirely natural and positive reaction; a self-protective, instinctive response to danger. At its most basic, it alerts us to something that is potentially life-threatening, and it prepares the body to have the strength to deal with it, either by taking on-the-spot action, or by running away (the 'fight or flight' response). It occurs in all animals, and it is massively important if we find ourselves face to face, for example, with a charging bull or a runaway truck. If we didn't experience the emotion of fear, we would be unable to protect ourselves from genuine life-or-death scenarios.

If your life is currently in danger

There are, of course, many different levels of fear. *If you fear that your life is genuinely in danger right now, then please remove yourself to a safe place and get help before you do anything else. Find a safe space* and talk things through with a trusted person until the immediate threat has passed. You can return to this book when the imminent danger has subsided, but please put yourself out of danger first. For important sources of help in this situation, see Appendix 3.

The many faces of fear

This is our body's primary defence mechanism and because it is so important to our survival it is the shortest neural circuit in the brain; the biological response that kicks in fastest when we are under any threat or stress. But the system doesn't distinguish between the fear when a roaring tiger is charging towards us, compared to, say, the fear of how we will pay our bills. It's all fear as far as the brain is concerned. Hence the chemicals which flood our body and cause us to feel so strange are also activated when we have fears of a less life-threatening nature.

Why is this important to know? Because when you are feeling broken, despairing, or at a very low point in your life, there will be some measure of fear woven into your story, whether you are aware of it or not. Other emotions may feel more prominent for you but there will also be fear, even if you don't name it as such. Fear of what this means for your future. Fear of how you will cope. Financial fears. Health fears. Relationship fears. Many aspects of fear that are both normal and completely understandable.

Most of us have some level of fear underpinning our inner wounds. Will anyone understand? Will people still love me if I tell them the truth? What if these feelings never go away? Sometimes we fear the reactions of others and how those reactions will make us feel. Mostly we fear whether we can cope with our own difficult feelings. Author and Episcopal priest Barbara Brown Taylor writes, 'Almost everyone is afraid of being afraid.'[26]

The phrase 'Do not fear' occurs often in the Bible. It's a recommended strategy for a healthy life. But it can be easier said than done. Fear can paralyse us. When fear is all-pervasive it can hold us in its grip and make us close in on ourselves. It can be so dominant, even subconsciously, that we begin to see everything through the lens of our fears and every action we take is driven by them. As Dr Simon Walker, founder of STEER Education,[27] a ground-breaking organisation to track and improve student mental health, says, 'However fear resides within us, its impact is always the same. We are left diminished by its presence, reduced from the people we could be.'[28]

Fear is the cause of all those weird sensations; palpitations, shakiness, upset tummy and all the rest. You will only be able to find a healthy way through your situation once you have first settled those unpleasant sensations in your body. We will look at ways to help you to do that.

Bottled-up energy

Fear, then, is both natural and necessary. But once the danger has passed, if that fear isn't released, that's when it becomes a problem. If we don't discharge the energy of the fear, if we bottle it up, it gets locked within the cells of our body and colours our future reactions to other traumas in unhealthy ways, even if those subsequent traumas are much less severe. The energy of the original fear doesn't go away. Although we may be unaware of it, it becomes trapped in our nervous system and can have physical, as well as behavioural, impacts. The body becomes the hiding place of our pain.

Research is now uncovering the understanding that 'holding on to fear' is one of the main culprits behind chronic anxiety and many chronic illnesses, including cancer.[29] Fear is a form of energy and any energy that builds up inside something needs at some point to be discharged to re-establish nature's healthy balance. Lightning streaking across the sky is powerfully discharging built-up electrostatic energy from the clouds. When a volcano erupts it is releasing a build-up of magma and gas from deep within the earth. Any form of energy can only build for so long before its pressure pops.

This need for energy to be released is true of good energy too. On a warm summer evening in 2012, I vividly remember watching the last night of the London Olympics. A small, wiry man was running round a track, carefully maintaining his place among a group of other athletes. They were all keeping in step with each other, until the start of the final lap, when everything changed. As if at the flick of a switch, Mo Farah accelerated his stride to a blistering pace and surged ahead. As he powered himself effortlessly across the finish line to claim Olympic gold, the entire stadium erupted in a riot of celebration. Every Briton was on their feet, waving their Union Jacks and cheering as if their life depended on it.[30] His victory crowned a wonderful night at London 2012. The Olympic crowd's wild enthusiasm was also, like the lightning storm, an example of a discharge of tension: in this case, an emotional build-up of joy.

Tensions always need to be released before they do harm.

Nature's way

The body is good at telling us when all is not well. Fear has its own powerful energy and when we fail to release it the bottled-up energy will eventually express itself in struggle and pain, in illness, anxiety and a whole host of other conditions. Animals naturally discharge this energy once the threat has passed, usually by shaking. Ducks, after they have quarrelled, will flap their wings intensely, then go calmly on their way as if nothing had happened. They are releasing the pent-up energy of the stressful encounter. Even more dramatically, a gazelle which has just survived a life-threatening chase by a cheetah will shake so violently that its entire body goes into convulsions. Once the crisis has passed, animals successfully discharge their fear energies in this instinctive way. But we humans often don't. Sometimes we will powerfully shake when we are on the other side of the danger, and occasionally while we are in the thick of the crisis. But it doesn't always happen.

Our nervous systems are programmed to release the energy through shaking or tears, but we humans tend to override that automatic response and take control of our reaction. In other words, we suppress what naturally wants to happen. This is exactly how the fear gets held inside us. Ironically, in an adult, this is usually due to other fears and to cultural conditioning. It results from us telling ourselves things like 'boys don't cry', 'I don't want to appear weak', or similar thought processes we have absorbed from those around us. Fear often gets held inside a child because they don't know how to process the event that has frightened them.

Animals shake the fear off. We often suppress it, and that causes us ongoing problems.

The Bible tells us that 'perfect love expels all fear'[31] and the only perfect love is that of God. Does this mean that trusting in God's love can help us to overcome all fears? Yes, my experience is that it can, as we deepen our relationship with God. Jesus said, 'Don't be afraid. Just have faith.'[32] Sounds easy to say and much harder to do, doesn't it? First, you need to uncover what it is that you fear. You may be able to name that straightaway. Or you may not.

> ## Pause Point

Naming your fears

Another way to help yourself settle into stillness is to repeat a word or phrase. Saying the name 'Jesus' acts as an invitation for Jesus to be with you.

Find a quiet spot.

You might find it helpful to close to your eyes after you have read these instructions.

Then calm yourself with some long, slow breaths.

Let your breathing settle into its natural rhythm and repeat the name 'Jesus' with each breath. Match the 'Je' to the in-breath and the 'sus' to the out-breath so that you are breathing the name of Jesus. Je-sus. Je-sus.

When you have quietened yourself in this way, ask Jesus to show you what it is that you fear.

Keep breathing steadily and wait. Don't stress. Just wait.

It's unlikely that you'll hear an audible voice, but an answer may pop into your thoughts.

It can be helpful to then ask yourself the question, 'Why do I fear that?'

Journal any insight that has emerged.

If you have someone supporting you (a friend, pastor or therapist, for instance), explore your fears with them.

CHAPTER 4

Defusing Your Emotions

The heart heals itself when it's open to pain.
Miriam Greenspan[33]

Suppressed emotions control us,
while expressed emotions heal and free us.
Niki Hardy[34]

The turbulent landscape

With a degree in philosophy and a doctorate in neuroscience, Sam Harris writes widely about the interface between spirituality, neuroscience and psychology. As he observes, 'Normal isn't necessarily a happy place to be.'[35] Whatever life circumstances have led you to this point, any sense of brokenness you have is being driven by your thoughts and by your emotions. Emotions are both wonderful and powerful things. They are an extraordinary gift. Without them how would we experience the deep joy of holding a new little life in our arms, or the sense of wonder at seeing the beauty of the first snowdrops bursting to life through the rock-hard ground of winter? How could we adequately express the warmth of love, the sadness of loss, or the joy of success? Our emotions are an extraordinary facet of what it means to be human.

But they have their difficult side too. There are emotions we feel less comfortable with. They enable us, on the other end of the emotional spectrum, to experience anger, bitterness, fear, hatred, grief and sometimes, overwhelming despair. None of us want to experience such feelings. But they happen. They surge up unbidden when painful things happen in our lives. They are part of us. They aren't 'wrong' or 'bad'; they are simply normal reactions to challenging situations, activated by our amazing neurological systems. But they don't feel good, and we certainly don't like feeling them.

We are sold the story of a 'happy ever after' world and, in our hearts, it is what we all aspire to. Why wouldn't we want to? It is what a multi-million-pound advertising industry is built on and what drives the growth in self-help books of every kind. It is what motivates us to climb the career ladder, to earn more money, to find the perfect partner and to be continually searching for an elusive perfect happiness that we hope to arrive at somewhere in the unknown future. To quote the psychotherapist Miriam Greenspan: 'We all want to sit at the happiness banquet and feast on the bread of contentment, the wine of joy. We'd rather skip the emotional food that doesn't go down so well.'[36]

Facing the feelings

Facing our wounds head-on can be a very painful process and we generally prefer not to do it. We become masters at running from them. We reach for the wine or the chocolate, turn on the television or pick up the iPhone. Some indulge in sex, drug-taking, or self-harm. Others bury themselves in busyness or frantic exercise. Anything rather than face the pain. By temporarily distracting ourselves from the unhappiness, we imagine it will go away. But it won't. Suppressing our hurts will never bring us lasting peace. It will simply be like trying to cover up a deep wound with a sticking plaster. In addition, the strategies we adopt to avoid processing our feeling can, over time, create a bigger problem than the problem we were trying to avoid. 'The more we run from our feelings the more they will run us',[37] as psychologist Gail Brenner writes.

One of the keys to beginning to feel well again is to begin to face our emotions with love and curiosity. That probably sounds counterintuitive, but it is one of the most helpful things we can do. Emotions and physical feelings in the body are related. By observing the sensations gently, instead of trying to resist or suppress them, we can relax the tensions in the cells and dissipate the emotion. We must show love to those weird feelings we'd rather not be experiencing.

The junk drawer

Every house has one. Mine is in the kitchen. The junk drawer. That place where you throw all the things that you are sure you'll need one day but don't quite know what to do with right now. That old penknife your father gave you. The giveaway book of matches with the hotel logo. Assorted pens, most of which don't work. A bunch of keys you have long since forgotten about. The odd receipt that felt important at the time. Tape, magnets, safety pins, rubber bands. The junk drawer is home to a whole cacophony of objects that accumulate around family life. It's the drawer where we throw things that we don't have the time or inclination to deal with immediately. We tell ourselves we are keeping things tidy, but the reality is we are storing up trouble for the future. For when the day comes when we urgently need that radiator key, or the business card the plumber gave us months ago, the contents of the junk drawer are by then in such a state that it is impossible to unearth said items. Meanwhile there is water cascading all over the best carpet and tempers are getting somewhat frayed. You get the gist. Things get stuffed away when we don't make time to deal with them, and sometimes there are consequences further down the line.

You may have been distracting yourself from your emotions for some time and unknowingly internalising them both physically and mentally. You may have been stuffing them in the 'emotional junk drawer' until they have become a complex tangle that is incredibly hard to sift through. It might now be almost impossible to answer the 'how are you feeling' question other than by saying, 'I'm in a mess.'

When we ignore emotions, they don't go away. Our pain hides within the cells of our body. Every time we suppress our feelings we metaphorically stuff them in the junk drawer of our cells. We don't realise we are doing it, but that is what happens. Unprocessed emotions never die. They live on within the cells of the body and cause changes which feel uncomfortable and can lead to all manner of health issues.

Releasing the cellular tensions is crucial to our healing, but we rarely make that our highest priority, other than to perhaps talk to a doctor about how strange we feel. The relentless noise in our heads tends to be so great that we naturally assume that sorting that out will lead us to the solution to our problems. In part that's true. But it isn't the whole picture.

The weird and uncomfortable sensations we experience are caused by that natural burst of chemicals which are preparing our body to counter a threat. Any threat, large or small. This happens whether we are in fear of losing our life or are frightened about something quite different, like how we will pay the mortgage, or where we will live if the landlord evicts us, or what divorce will mean for our children. A similar response can happen with all the fears which emerge in the early stages of grief; fears like how we will cope and what this loss means for us.

What do we do with this fear energy which gets locked inside our body if we don't release it? There are two primary ways to 'unlock' it. Sometimes it is appropriate to discharge it physically. At other times the best thing to do is to observe the sensations in our body with loving attention.

The angry way

Some emotions have an intense energy to them, and that form of energy is best discharged in a physical way. Anger, for instance, is a flashing red warning light from our nervous system; an impossible to ignore signal that our life has somehow been violated in an intolerable and unjustified way. It is an intense inner tension in the cells of our body, shouting at us that 'this is wrong'.

It's an emotion with an urgency to it and we feel it in our guts, in the tightening of our muscles, in the change of our heart rhythm, in the tight grip in our skull. The flood of sensations surging through our body demands to be heard. It's an intense physical tension that needs a physical release. Which, of course, is exactly how punch-ups start. In one moment of anger whole lives can be ruined, which is entirely why we must process anger in a safe way. Retaliation is never a good thing. It simply adds fuel to the fire of an already inflamed situation, yet all our instincts may be to react by lashing out, even if only verbally.

It is vital that you process anger safely; not by directing the energy at the person who provoked it. Punch your pillow, do some vigorous exercise that helps you work off your rage, go to the woods and scream it all out, or pour it all out onto paper and then rip it up aggressively. Do something physical to discharge the energy and allow your cells to return to a more relaxed state. Find a way to channel and express the intensity of your anger without causing further hurt to anyone else.

Throwing stones

I threw stones once. Lots of them.

My husband walked out of our marriage of twenty-seven years. The pain of his leaving was immense. It felt as if the heart had been ripped out of our family. Once the initial shock had subsided, my primary emotion was anger; an anger that I knew I had to process safely.

I took myself off to the countryside and marched angrily down a secluded track, stomping through puddles, letting the tensions build within me. I scanned the ground for stones, my mind noisily rehearsing all I wanted to say. Stone after grubby stone got unceremoniously stuffed into the pockets of my jacket. With each one I felt the weight of it, fingered the roughness of it, paused to recall the injustice and pain it represented for me. Stomp, stomp. Another stone. Another memory. Another anger recalled. When my pockets could hold no more, I filled my rucksack. The heaviness of the bag mirrored the heaviness in my heart. Tears flowed with each new rock that I added.

Later, rounding a bend, a lake came into view. Fringed and overhung by trees on three sides, I was immediately struck by its seclusion. Wild irises sprung up on the far side of the lake, while marsh marigolds grew and blossomed around the edge. Dragonflies hovered in the air, and all was still. It was a little oasis in a clearing.

I chose a spot at one end and emptied out my collection. Big stones, small stones, rough ones, smooth ones: they all tumbled out at my feet. I stood there, picked up the first one, breathed deeply and threw it with all the energy I could muster. I was so angry with God. With each stone, I voiced the anger it represented and flung it into the lake. I had no idea I had so much pain inside me. Another stone. Another memory. More angry words. Another splash. Until it was done. Finally, exhausted, I sank to my knees by the water's edge and simply watched the ripples dying away, until the surface of the lake was mirror-still again.

The anger was gone. It had been released.

The tears of grief

Grief is another emotion which carries a heavy intensity with it, especially in the early days following bereavement or loss. As with anger, it is hugely important to give ourselves permission to let the tears surge through us when they need to, and to resist the temptation to feel that we should be 'over this' by now.

I was unexpectedly plunged into another season of intense and profound grief during the latter stages of writing this book. A family tragedy rocked my world, and I needed to cling tightly to all that I have written of in these pages.

I gave myself permission to stop. To stop and to rest. To stop trying to power on like Superwoman. I needed to lay down the writing of this book, and all my other projects, and show kindness to the distress surfacing in my body. To practise resting my mind in my 'Stillness Spot'. The reality was that I could do no other.

Everyone deals with grief differently. Sometimes we are so caught up in the practicalities of the situation we are dealing with that we are unable to give ourselves the luxury of stopping, to allow the underlying grief to flow through us. It's just not possible in that moment. But for some, this becomes a long-term coping strategy; a distraction from fully facing the depth of our feelings. We bury our feelings because we unconsciously feel that we will 'break' if we don't keep busy.

But, at some point, stop we must. When my grieving got to the point where I was struggling to function, I stopped. I laid everything down and gave priority to taking a prolonged pause. I used all the practices in this book and allowed myself to simply 'sit' with my grief and let its first powerful tsunami run its course. Mainly, I sat by my favourite lake and let the stillness and green space of nature begin to heal me. I sat there often, for days and weeks, until the tears gradually morphed into gentler, intermittent waves of sadness.

The grieving process is different for every individual and rarely follows a well-defined path. Grieving takes as long as it takes. In time, we may move from the acute stage of our grief to a point at which sadness and related emotions surface more sporadically. That is the time to treat those emotions and feelings in the gentle way.

The gentle way: Love over fear

With less intense emotions there is a more compassionate way. We need to somehow show love to those weird feelings which we would rather not be experiencing. With gentle observation we can soften any emotion and the feelings that accompany it. Love can particularly defuse our fears.

I was reminded of that recently. Walking along the canal, I was observing the narrowboats. I love their traditional paintwork with its panoply of colours, and I am fascinated by the names people give them. One which caught my eye was *Love Over Fear*. It's an unusual name for a boat. And I wondered what led the owner of that boat to paint those words on the gunwale.

Love over fear.

Those three little words resonate with a truth that we all need to hear. They remind me of the teachings of Swiss-American psychiatrist Elisabeth Kübler-Ross, who pioneered studies in death and dying and transformed the care of the terminally ill. In her writings, she states that the two emotions of love and fear simply cannot coexist together.[38] They are like oil and water. We are either driven by feelings based on fear, or those that are firmly rooted in love. And love can overcome fear. Any fear. In fact, it is probably the only thing that can.

The ninety-second surprise

Being aware of your emotions and being tender with them will help you to heal; you will be exercising love over fear. When an emotion gets triggered, as I have said, your brain releases a wave of chemicals which flush through your body and result in unusual sensations. It is just that: a wave. When you can learn to ride the wave, as a surfer does on the ocean, the wave will pass. Now here's the surprising bit: the rush of chemicals lasts a maximum of ninety seconds and then dissipates. It is very similar to the way a wave on the shoreline lingers for a moment before it subsides.[39]

It may well be your experience that a surge of emotion always seems to last much longer than a minute and a half. That will be the case if you fight against the feeling or attach a negative story to it. Struggling with the feeling will perpetuate it by launching another wave of chemicals. Then another, and another, and another, so that the emotion simply persists.

The secret is to stay present to the experience, ride the ninety-second wave, and let the sensations run their course. To nestle, not wrestle. If you sit with the feelings, observe them, and let them be, they *will* die out quickly and this will help you to heal. If you practise this often, the tensions in your cells will begin to ease, the unpleasant sensations will lessen, and you will begin to feel much better. This is about letting the emotions flow unhindered and simply observing them, without attaching a story to them. It is about letting them be, as you sit with them quietly and, as you do that, noticing that in time the waves of emotion slowly settle into a naturally calm place. It will be a tired place, but a calm place. And that is where you can sometimes become aware that somehow, mysteriously, you are held in the embrace and comfort of God.

This can feel very counterintuitive, but it works. Our feelings simply want to be felt, not suppressed. If you can hold your emotions in awareness and love, that will be a key part of your healing. Soften the feeling in the cells of your body and you will soften your pain. Remember that principle with this mnemonic:

Hold your **E**motions in **A**wareness and **L**ove

Try to get into the habit of pausing, every time you become aware of an emotion rising to the surface in you. The pause is important; without it you will find yourself reacting in unhelpful ways. After the pause, practise the exercise below. The more you can get into the habit of reacting in this way, the more effective it will become, and the easier life will begin to feel.

Pause Point

Holding your emotions in awareness and love

Close your eyes after you have read these instructions.

Start with a prayer, asking God to be with you.

Bring yourself to stillness with one of the simple breathing exercises you learned earlier.

As you sit in silence, become aware of any unusual bodily sensations.

Just notice them and accept them.

Don't attach a storyline to them and don't fight them.

With each inhale, gently breathe into that part of your body.

Stay focused and aware, as if you are looking at the sensations with curiosity.

Keep breathing into them, repeating this for as long as you need to.

Be kind to the feelings and they will dissipate, just like a wave dies on the shore.

Keep breathing into that area until you notice that the wave has passed.

As you continue to sit in silence, let the tension and stress in the cells of your body begin to naturally be released.

CHAPTER 5

The Inner Story

Change your thinking and you change your life.
Cynthia Curry[40]

Pain is inevitable; suffering is optional.[41]

More than we think we are

The biggest battles we face are always in our mind. Our brain is constantly searching for connections and striving to make meaning of what is happening within us and around us. When our world is upended or blown apart, our head can become the ultimate battleground. Because the voice that we listen to most is always the one in our own head, the one that may be repeating all the negative stuff about the situation we find ourselves in. An undercurrent of negative thoughts can become so embedded in us that we are hardly aware of it.

What keeps us in a bad place is, almost always, the way that we are thinking about things. That's particularly true when we are making a set of circumstances mean something about ourselves. For instance, if I have the misfortune to be involved in a serious car accident, I might find myself thinking that 'it was my fault because I am a dangerous driver, and I shouldn't be behind the wheel'. That might then lead me to limit my life by giving up driving completely. And that reactive thought at the time of the accident might not be true. There may have been multiple other factors at play, but I have made the incident mean something about me.

There is always a wider picture.

Just because something bad has happened in your life it does not mean that there is anything inherently wrong or unlovable about you. We are always more than our thoughts seem to be telling us we are. We were not born thinking anything bad about ourselves. It is only the things that have happened in life that have changed our perception of what we think about ourselves and the world. Beneath all the layers of experience, the perfect essence of the newborn 'you' is still who you are at your core. And furthermore, you can have within you all the resources you need to navigate life's struggles, through the presence and power of the Holy Spirit. When you can learn to let go of the negative voices that are unconsciously driving your behaviour, everything can begin to change.

The anatomy of suffering

There is a difference between suffering and pain. Difficult emotions arise naturally when the brain responds, unbidden and instantaneously, to situations that feel in some way threatening. All this is a healthy part of our inbuilt survival mechanisms. So, difficult feelings and emotions will arise. Often. We all feel pain.

Suffering is different. Suffering arises from believing we cannot be at peace until our situation becomes the way we want it to be. It occurs when our ideas about how things ought to be, or how we 'deserve' them to be, don't match how they really are. It perpetuates itself when our perception of events, which may be more distorted than we realise, cycles relentlessly in our head. As the quote at the start of this chapter says:

> Pain is inevitable; suffering is optional.

In the thick of our struggles, the pain we are living with can feel all-consuming. There's no escape from it. It is with us night and day, no matter how much we try to distract ourselves from it. We might enjoy brief glimmers of relative normality before it bounces back to demand our attention again. The brain is sending us a message that all is not well with our inner being and we need to respond. Until we begin to take some action the brain will keep shouting its 'help' message at us and we will feel trapped in a downhill spiral.

Beginning to understand what is happening within us can help us to find a way through. Because suffering is always more than just a set of complicated emotions and their associated strange bodily sensations. Wrapped around all this and compounding it is our inner narrative; the story we are telling ourselves about our pain. There is also the external situation that we are living this story out within. It's the combination of everything that makes us feel so unwell.

Several things are going on in this painful interplay between mind and body. Tensions from the pain we have failed to address earlier are held in the cells of our body and are giving rise to strange physical sensations. Our mind, meanwhile, is drowning in a whirlpool of difficult emotions. If we could simply accept both of those things, we would be well on the way to finding a measure of healing. But so often, we compound the situation by our mental commentary. As psychotherapist Miriam Greenspan points out, 'All life contains emotional pain. There's the pain; and there's the story we tell ourselves about it.'[42] Our head rehearses a constant story about why we are feeling as we are (usually to do with the way someone has mistreated us, words that have been spoken over us earlier in our life, the mistakes we have made, or the general undeserved unfairness of life). Each time that story cycles round in our brain it intensifies the pain, and we become locked deeper into the suffering place because we trigger another ninety-second wave of chemicals. And round and round goes the spiral of suffering.

The Inner Story

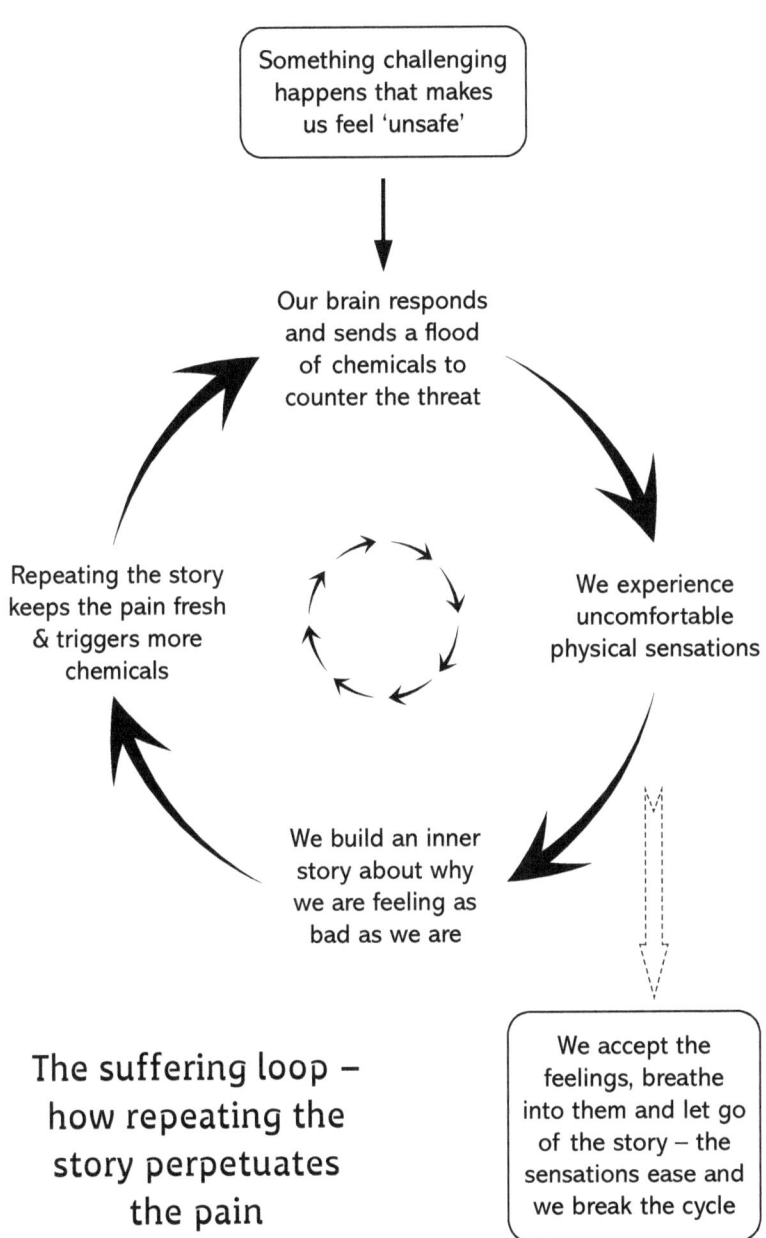

The stories we tell ourselves

Every situation of pain that we suffer with has an accompanying story that we tell ourselves; a dialogue that rattles round in our head. Unless we take evasive action, this inner story becomes increasingly dominant as we, very understandably, wrestle with thoughts about what led us to this dark and difficult place, whose 'fault' it was, and how on earth we can begin to change how we are feeling. The more the story relentlessly cycles, the more it holds us in the pain.

It might be an entirely plausible and valid train of thought. For example:

> 'I hate what he's done to me.'
> 'I'm never going to survive without...'
> 'She's ruined my life.'

Any number of similar phrases may have taken up residence in our head. It might seem like an entirely justified inner story but until we can let it go, it keeps us well and truly stuck inside the pain. We can get so locked into the constantly circulating narrative, the angry words that we are repeating in our head, that we simply cannot see beyond it. We are finding it desperately hard to think straight and all we can see is the worrying whirlpool of our struggles. It is as if we are viewing the world through blinkers and can see nothing but our painful story.

I observed this in someone recently.

Blind to wonder

With a coffee by my side, my iPad on the table and a peaceful view of my favourite lake before me, I was engrossed. Words flowed and I barely noticed the few other customers around me. It was the distinctive cry of birds that first distracted me, followed by the wingbeats of upwards of 100 geese on the move. Everyone lifted their eyes and turned their heads in one direction. Someone grabbed a camera. A child ran to the railing, eyes wide open, as if opening them wide was the only way to take in the wonder of what was unfolding. A flight of geese, looking like an enormous wave of miniature aircraft, was darkening the sky and powering in formation towards us. It was a stunning spectacle of nature.

Everyone was utterly captivated. All but for one person, who was sitting a few tables away from me. Immersed in relating an intense story of their problems to their companion, they were so totally preoccupied with their pain that they were completely oblivious to the wonder of what was taking place just a few feet away.

When we are in pain it's not uncommon to be so consumed by our thoughts that our mind is incapable of 'seeing' anything else.

Getting respite from the story

Paradoxically, we can't always see our inner dialogue clearly when we are in its grip. That's how it was for me one day: the commentary in my head simply would not stop. The story I was telling myself about my situation thundered round in my head, like a big ugly giant spoiling for a fight. It was relentless. It dulled my senses. It wore me down. It dragged me kicking and screaming into a deep, dark hole of depression and I felt powerless to stop it. I felt unable to function normally. Even to move from the chair felt is if it would require a gargantuan effort. I wanted to scream, but even that potential release felt locked inside me, unable to be voiced.

Sometimes the story of our inner pain makes itself felt like that: it can hold us in its grip. I wonder if you have ever experienced that? Have you discovered strategies that help you in such moments?

That day, I finally got myself out of the house; the space which felt so oppressive in that moment. I picked up the car keys and began to drive. I had no idea where I was going. I just knew that I needed to escape. To escape from my inner self. Even if only for a brief respite. As the engine began to hum and the familiar neural pathways kicked in, engaging my hands and feet with the business of steering and gear changing and all the peripheral activities of driving, something changed. My internal agony was no longer my only focus. My attention moved away from my problems; those thoughts which only a few minutes earlier had prompted me to want to scream. My body relaxed and softened. The tensions, which I had been unaware I was bracing myself with, relaxed. Half an hour later, I was sitting by the water of the marina, just soaking in the scene. Boats moored. Ducks preening themselves. Ripples on the water. The wide, open sky. Stillness, and the cool evening air on my skin. Finally, peace began to gently nudge its way into my soul.

I had stopped overthinking the struggle. It would be necessary to revisit the pain and the problems later, but in that moment, as a swan glided serenely past, a pair of mallards circled overhead, and colours of evening began to paint the sky, the urgency of the struggle had passed. I had temporarily stilled the inner narrative. I had been able to press 'pause'.

To become aware of our inner dialogue we need to first step back from it, and we achieve that by whatever helps us to come to a stillness beyond the mental chatter, a stillness beyond ourselves. Only when we can quieten that insistent voice in our head can we begin to really explore how to change it. Only then can we avoid being caught in the spiral of suffering.

There are many ways we can be helped to do this. Getting out and about in nature is a perfect way. It is now widely accepted that time spent in nature can be enormously healing.

Pause Point

Stilling yourself in nature

Time in nature can be very healing.

If you are able to get out and about, take yourself, as I did, to somewhere where there is greenery: trees, flowers, nature, space.

If that's not possible, see if your eyes can simply rest on some aspect of nature that you can see through a window.

Let the sights and sounds around you just fill your senses, either walking slowly and rhythmically, or just sitting, looking and listening.

Observe, really observe, whatever is before you.

Be still. Simply look.

Resist the temptation to name what you see. Just look.

Notice the colours, the shapes, the textures, the way the light falls.

Listen to the sounds around you. Be aware of the silence beneath the sounds.

Reach out and touch something. Anything. Feel its texture. Be aware of the life running through it.

Use all your senses to be completely in this place, this moment.

Allow your eyes to wander. And to wonder.

Enjoy the experience.

Pray about what you've just experienced and how it has made you feel.

Pausing the struggle

The above will be a good first step. If you have managed to immerse yourself in those surroundings, hopefully you will have temporarily silenced the story of struggle which was looping round in your head.

You may feel tired afterwards and that's OK. Allow yourself to rest if you need to. The tiredness will be a delayed reaction to the inner wrestling which was going on before you chose to stop. We rarely notice it, but in the middle of our silent scream our body is often filled with tensions. It's only as we still the inner scream that the cells begin to relax. At that point, tiredness comes and that's good. Go with the flow. Let yourself have a nap. Or even a good long sleep. Rest is restorative. Healing takes place when you relax.

The struggle has not completely gone away. But for a few moments you have given your brain some respite from endlessly thinking about it, and you have also gained a new perspective: that there is beauty out there in the world. As contemplative photographer Steve Radley is fond of saying, 'Beauty is never more than a step away.'[43]

CHAPTER 6

New Perspectives

When you finally learn that a person's behaviour has more to do with their own internal struggle than it ever did with you, you learn grace.
Allison Aars [44]

We can complain because rose bushes have thorns or rejoice because thorn bushes have roses.[45]

Locked in the pain

So how do we break this cycle? How do we begin to change the inner narrative that is keeping us stuck in a never-ending loop of suffering? Two things can help: looking at things from a different angle and putting our inner story under the microscope.

Each time the words you are telling yourself cycle round again in your mind, it keeps your angry story alive and deepens your pain. Because it is so often a story about blame or regret, about whose fault it was and how you could have avoided being in this dark, unhappy place if another person or group of people, or even yourself, had behaved differently. Repeating the story perpetuates the pain. Replacing that mental dialogue with a new inner story is one of the things that will help you to dissipate the pain and move forward. But how? How can you do that? Looking at things from a different angle will help. You may need support to explore this with someone, or you may find different viewpoints emerge when you honestly look at your situation.

Every single person, in every moment, has a reason for behaving in the way that they do. They may not even be consciously aware of what that reason is. But there will be a reason. I know that is incredibly hard to hear if someone has let you down badly or wounded you in some way, but it's true. Hurting people hurt others, even innocently. None of us are perfect and all of us are living out our life under the influence of our own wounds and disappointments. Everyone is carrying some unhealed pain. That's true of you. It's true of me. It's also true of everyone associated with your current unhappiness. When we are hurting deeply, it is easy to be oblivious to the possibility that the other participants in our drama might be struggling too. Inevitably they will be. But we are often hurting too much to be able to see or acknowledge that.

Cathy Madavan writes, 'We create perceptions of others, but we don't always know what battles they may have faced.'[46] That can even be true of those whom we have spent the whole of our lives with. Everyone has past experiences, good and bad, which have shaped them. Your past experiences have shaped you. And mine have shaped me.

No matter how hard it was for you to be on the receiving end, no matter how much you may feel like a victim, everyone else who contributed to your current state of mind was also living out of their own struggles. That doesn't make what they did right. It doesn't take away your pain. But perhaps it helps you to see the situation more compassionately. Perhaps everyone was doing the best they were capable of at the time?

Once you have processed the initial depths of your pain, it is essential to take your attention off the perpetrators of the things that have upset you. Shifting your viewpoint can help you to stop fighting your feelings. It can help you to be tender with the feelings and look at them in a new light, being as gentle with yourself as you would be with someone else.

A different angle

I first met Steve Radley when I took part in a contemplative photography retreat, entitled 'Seeing with the eyes of the heart'. It was a photography event with a difference. It was a real awakening into how stilling oneself and seeing things with deep awareness can be life-changing. Steve had personally used contemplative photography to help him to heal from trauma in the aftermath of military service in Afghanistan. This is not dissimilar to all I have written about the benefits of taking time to be mindfully aware in nature as a practice for stilling your mind and sensing the presence of God in all things. The only difference was that on our retreat we had a camera in our hand.

One important photography skill that we were encouraged to experiment with was looking at things from a different angle. I had photographed the ornamental bird bath already. Most of us had. But my shot was the conventional view that I got as I was walking towards it. Armed with Steve's instructions to try to see things in a new way, I revisited this area of the garden and took a variety of photographs from different angles. Towards the sun, through the leaves of some foliage, focusing on the detail of the stonework, lying on the ground and looking upwards, picturing it from above. Later, when I browsed through the images, I was struck by how much I had missed by just looking at the bird bath in one way. Looking at the object from different perspectives opened my eyes to a host of realities which I had never considered before.

What we know from quantum theory is that how we look at things affects what we believe we see.[47] What is true in quantum physics and what I discovered through my photography exercise is also very important on the healing journey, especially when the inner story we are telling ourselves keeps looping round on repeat. There is always another way of looking at things, but when we are in a bad place it can be hard to see. How you look at things affects what you see. For example, when you look at people through the lens of 'they don't care' you see people not caring. When you look at life through the lens of 'fear' you see things to be afraid of. And so on.

How you look at things will go a long way to determining how you heal from the wounds you have gathered along life's way.

The telephoto lens

Another thing I love about photography is being able to zoom in on the subject with a telephoto lens. The details we would often otherwise miss can teach us so much. It can be helpful to zoom in on your mental commentary in a similar way. To take time to examine the detail of what you are constantly saying to yourself. Not in a judgmental way, but in a curious way, as you would when looking through a viewfinder. It wasn't easy to look at that bird bath from a different angle. I had to work at it, get down on my knees, explore all the different possibilities and think outside the box. But the results were so worth it.

Beneath the level of our conscious awareness, nearly every waking moment of our lives, we are living out of an inner story that has been formed by our past. And this inner narrative influences how we feel in any given situation that we encounter. To help us make sense of what is happening, our brain brings old memories to the surface; memories which are related to what we are experiencing in that instant. When those are memories of painful experiences, they often have a story attached to them; one that we have unknowingly carried with us throughout our life. This is often part of the inner narrative that is keeping us locked in suffering.

Let's look at those words that keep repeating in your head; the ones that make you feel tense, or bitter, or frustrated. The words that are screaming out at you again and again as you try to get on with life. The words that, without you realising it, are judging the situation, or maybe even casting judgement on yourself. The words that are your voice of inner desperation. They probably won't be nice words. But that's OK. They are your words. And you are saying them to yourself. Often.

Let's do it now. Pick up that pen and get your notebook. Put the kettle on and come back when you are ready.

Pause Point

Zooming in on the story

Bring yourself to a place of stillness in whatever way works for you. Maybe have a few moments of awareness: just closing your eyes, breathing slowly and noticing all the sounds around you and within you. Or noticing the sensations in your body as the air flows in and out through your nostrils. Or consciously breathing out tensions and breathing in peace. If you choose to do this outside, just sit for a few moments simply observing everything you can see, seeing it in all its detail and taking in the wonder of it all. If you have found the practice of

New Perspectives

silence helpful, you could just close your eyes for a few moments of total quiet.

Ask God to be with you.

When you are in that still, calm place, ask yourself the question, 'What are the phrases that keep echoing in my head?'

Take some time to become aware of them, without judgement. There might be just one dominant phrase that you repeat to yourself, or there might be two or three.

When you know what they are, write down the main one. Write it in big, bold letters.

You will probably notice a tension in your body as you see the words written out big and bold. That's OK. These are difficult words for you. They are part of your pain.

Just take a few calming breaths, then carry on.

Sit with this for a while until you are ready to return to this book.

Your response

So now you have your dominant, repetitive phrase written in big, bold letters in your notebook. Those words are your response to what has happened to you. No more, no less. Everyone else involved in your circumstances will see things slightly differently.

Only you see things as you see them. No matter how altruistic you are, you will always, first and foremost, see the effect that things are having on yourself. We all do. The words in front of you, therefore, are not so much the full facts of the situation but rather the interpretation that you have placed on your version of events; the way in which the situation has affected you. That's not a criticism; simply an observation.

Now take some time to work with the questions below. There are no right or wrong answers, only the answers that are true for you today. I am inviting you to 'zoom in', as with a telephoto lens, to get a better impression of what is deep within your repetitive inner commentary. It might be helpful to write out your responses in your journal.

Pause Point

Cross-examining the story

- **If the statement is about yourself: is it true?**
  Do I really think this or am I repeating words that someone else used to say to me? You may have absorbed a criticism of yourself that was never valid in the first place. This can be especially true of things that were said to you in your childhood. It can also be true of the interpretation your child-self put on a difficult experience. Can you link the

words back to such a memory? Are the words true? Can you let them go?

- **Is it a criticism of someone else?** Much as we might prefer it to be otherwise, the only person we can change is ourselves. Voicing harsh words in your head about someone else will have no effect on them; it will only keep you locked in a cycle of pain by giving head space to something you cannot change. Can you let the words go?

- **Is there a fear underlying the story you keep repeating in your head?** If so, what is that fear? Can you trust in God's love to look after you instead of allowing yourself to be gripped by that fear?

- **Is it helping you to keep repeating this phrase in your head?** The longer you let those words rattle round in your mind, the longer it will take you to become free of them. Perhaps it's time to let them go; to replace them now with a new story?

Finding the positives

Having explored those questions, you may have come to the realisation that though you are speaking those words to yourself often, that inner narrative is not helping you to move forward. It is one of the things that is keeping you stuck in the pain. It will be helpful to talk through your responses with whoever is supporting you through your healing journey. No matter how justified or real those words feel, they are perpetuating your pain.

However bad your current circumstances are, there will always, always be something to be thankful for. You need to look with fresh eyes and identify the blessings of your situation. Life can be hard. Terribly hard, sometimes. But whatever situation you are facing, there will be some positives to be found as you emerge on the other side of the worst of it. Look for them and find them. An attitude of gratitude will get you through many of life's hurdles. It gives you that different viewpoint. As pastor and theologian Dietrich Bonhoeffer says, 'It is only with gratitude that life becomes rich.'[48]

A new inner story

Take some time to notice the things, however tiny, that you can give thanks for. How can you turn the words you are so often repeating to yourself into positive ones? Choose to make positive and life-affirming words the ones that circulate in your head. Better still, choose a phrase from Scripture. Make those words your new mantra. Decide to think differently and let that old story go. Make that commitment to yourself and share it with a trusted friend.

And whenever you catch yourself saying those old negative phrases, pull yourself up short and speak out an empowering thought instead. Rehearse it in your head, often. Write it in your notebook in letters as equally big and bold as that old phrase you just unearthed. Stick it on Post-it notes. Make it your new screensaver. Practise telling yourself your new inner story and it will gradually become your reality. This new phrase will be another weapon in your arsenal of recovery.

CHAPTER 7

The Question of Forgiveness

Forgiving is the only thing that can transform the aching wounds and the searing pain of loss.
Archbishop Desmond Tutu [49]

Forgiveness is healing.
Russ Parker [50]

The challenge of forgiveness

Some of this inner wounding is hard to let go of. We can throw stones, talk it all through, quieten our minds with stillness. We can invite Jesus in, be kind to our feelings, begin to pray, and all those things help. But there is still that story that is rattling round in our head. The blame story.

I hope you can see now that any blame story is keeping you in the pain and holding you back from healing. At some stage, it is necessary to accept that other people were acting out of their own inner wounds and history, which you may have known nothing about. The fact that they caused you hurt in some way means that they themselves were shouldering deep inner struggles of their own. Or it may be that you are placing the blame on yourself for the way in which you behaved. Either way, it is essential, for your own future wellbeing, to let the 'blame story' go. And one way to begin to lay it to rest is to forgive. To forgive others and to forgive yourself. Indeed, forgiveness is so important to our wholeness that it features in the most familiar prayer of all, the one Jesus taught his disciples to pray; the Lord's Prayer.[51]

Forgiveness can play a large part in cementing your eventual healing and in helping you to find peace. But 'forgiving' can feel a very big and daunting word; a place you maybe don't feel able to go to. It can be a struggle – sometimes a huge struggle. To even contemplate it may feel overwhelming to begin with, especially if you have experienced some shattering life event or some extreme childhood trauma. And that's completely normal. If you find it impossible right now, that's totally understandable and completely OK. You might not always feel that way.

When we can begin to do the hard work of forgiveness, it will help us to deepen our healing and find a new freedom from all that weighs heavily on us. But it isn't usually the first thing to happen on our healing journey. The willingness and desire to forgive, as Susan Atkinson writes, is 'more likely to grow as we heal emotionally and come to terms with what has happened to us'.[52] Exercising forgiveness is both the hardest thing and the best thing we can do, but it can only happen at the appropriate time in our healing journey, when we have processed the depth of our emotions. Very few of us can do it immediately. It's often a process. And it needs to be. We need to properly feel our grief and our anger before we can forgive.

Setting ourselves free

Suffering is a complicated mix of the things which have wounded us, the pain that has stirred in us and the tangle of thoughts and fears bound up with our situation. It can involve people whose actions or lack of actions have damaged us, connections to earlier life experiences and sometimes accidents or tragedies for which there is no one person to blame. Whatever the cause, our wounds will find expression in our inner anger towards someone or something, or even towards God. Sometimes we blame ourselves.

Amid the actual event that damages us, we get flooded with sensations and emotions that stir up our inner world and make us feel so uncomfortable that we can't help but react defensively. These arise primarily from our unconscious thoughts about the situation. Placing the blame elsewhere brings temporary relief to the dis-ease which arises in our body, and this defensive reaction is almost automatic. It's a reaction of the moment and for the moment. Few of us can stop it. But if we allow that response to stay with us long-term, the initial dis-ease can develop into more prolonged disease within our body. It can manifest itself as illness. Forgiveness can be pivotal on the steady journey to healing.

While we still carry resentment or bitterness towards another, we remain tethered to that person and their behaviour towards us is locked into our consciousness. It won't go away. It is constantly there and poisons our mind and our body with a pervasive discomfort. It imprisons us and we can find no peace from it. We wound ourselves by continuing to carry these festering feelings and yet our thoughts and feelings are making no difference at all to the other person. Nelson Mandela, speaking about the moment he was released after twenty-seven years in prison, said, 'As I walked out the door toward the gate that would lead to my freedom, I knew if I didn't leave my bitterness and hatred behind, I'd still be in prison.'[53] Jesus had something to say about this too. At the start of his ministry, he said that he had come to set prisoners free.[54]

Until we forgive someone, the wound that they inflicted on us remains a part of our thinking, rattling round in our head and possibly getting louder and more intense. Our mind keeps repeating its story about the offence and cannot let it go because the brain is still trying to find resolution to the injustice. It destroys us from the inside out. It subconsciously influences how we see everything else in our life.

The radical love that sets us free

Forgiveness is the way out of this prison. And Jesus holds the key.

Jesus loves you with a crazy love. Accepting that you are deeply loved by God, no matter how hard that might be to grasp, can change everything. Jesus demonstrated the depth of that love when he walked the earth 2,000 years ago. He led people to healing wherever he went. And Jesus still heals people today.

You might want to read that statement again: Jesus still heals people today.

Forgiveness is one of the ways in which Jesus brings about healing. This is not the place for an in-depth explanation of how and why that came to be possible. Simply put, Jesus died to set us free from all our guilt, especially from those things that we might find it incredibly hard to forgive ourselves for. And it was a painful death; crucified on a cross. On the night before he died, gathered around a meal table with his friends, holding up a cup of wine, he said:

> This is my blood, and with it God
> makes his agreement with you.
> It will be poured out so that many people
> will have their sins forgiven.[55]

You and I can be forgiven by God for anything and everything we have ever done wrong, provided we acknowledge those things and ask to be forgiven. Jesus shed his blood for us. For you. For me. For everyone. Can you imagine that? He allowed himself to be tortured on the cross so that you and I could have a close, forgiven relationship with God. And he did it because of his incredible love for us. Once you can get your head around that and know it deep in your guts, it's transformational. It's only when we fully realise how completely we are forgiven, and what Jesus went through to make that possible, that we can summon up the strength and the grace to forgive others.

Pause Point

Taking it all in

This is so important that you need to intentionally take time to take in the magnitude of what Jesus did for you.

Bring yourself to a place of stillness in your usual way.

Sit quietly for a moment.

When you are ready, if you feel you can, picture Jesus in your mind's eye, hanging on the cross.

Can you see the wounds on his body, the agony in his face? Can you see his blood trickling down the timbers of the cross?

Don't rush this. Sit with these images for as long as you feel able. Really see them. Feel them.

Can you take in the mystery that he went through this torture specifically for you?

If you feel able to, repeat these, or similar, words to yourself:

> Jesus died for me.
> He loves me so much that he willingly died on a cross for me.
> He died so that I can be forgiven.

Sit with your feelings as you consider how incredible that is.

Take in how amazing it is, how massive his love for you must be.

Let whatever wants to surface do so, then journal and pray with your thoughts.

Receiving God's forgiveness for yourself

The critical thing in your healing journey is being able to forgive the people who have wounded you. But that can be painfully hard. Before you try to forgive others, the most important first step is to know that you yourself are forgiven, whatever you have done or not done, said or not said. Whatever. Full stop. You can be forgiven by God. But sometimes the hardest person for you to forgive is yourself.

At least two streams of thinking may be churning within you as you wrestle with your pain. Almost always there is an anger with some person, persons or organisation that has caused your current state of distress. But equally, we are often angry with ourselves, sometimes for a multitude of reasons. So, the important questions become, not only can you forgive the 'other', but can you also stop blaming yourself? Can you let go of your pain and regrets relating to your own behaviour?

Whatever the cause of your pain, there will inevitably be things within it that you regret about yourself. We mentally beat ourselves up over our shortcomings and wrongdoings because we alone know our secrets and the behaviours we regret, the times when we wish we had acted differently or spoken kinder words. That knowledge eats away at us, the memories haunt us, we carry the tension of it all in the cells of our body, and we can never be fully at peace until we release those things.

Without forgiveness, our bad feelings can so easily become a dominant, consuming factor in our life, affecting everything we do, causing us to have a low opinion of ourselves and leading to serious consequences for our health. Ruminating on our regrets will never help us. We see God's heart to forgive demonstrated in the Bible, through Jesus. On one occasion, four people longed so deeply to see their paralysed friend healed that they lowered him through a roof so that he could get close to Jesus. It was obvious that his physical body was in need of healing, but the very first thing Jesus said to him was, 'Son, your sins are forgiven.'[56] Similarly, when a mob of angry men wanted to stone a woman caught in the act of adultery, Jesus himself did not condemn her.[57]

Jesus modelled forgiveness and, by pouring out his blood, made it available to everyone. Whenever we acknowledge our failures and wrongdoings, God will forgive us. He will forgive us totally. From everything. No questions asked. And that's healing. Incredibly healing. And when we can't say 'sorry' in any other way, we can say it to God.

Forgiving other people

Forgiving those who have wounded us is critical. But when we are suffering from deep hurts or loss, forgiving those involved in our woundedness can seem too overwhelming to even begin to contemplate. We may be hurting far too much to want to do that. How can we begin to forgive if the person involved shows no remorse? How can we consider it when there has been no reason given or explanation offered for their behaviour? And how do we forgive if we can't forget? Does forgiving mean that we excuse what happened; that it's somehow OK? Do we have to say it face to face? Where on earth do we start?

There is a natural tendency to want to get our own back when someone hurts us. It is completely normal to feel an aggressive response when what was done to us was wrong, unfair and undeserved. But it never helps. It will simply perpetuate a cycle of pain. The way to break that cycle is to forgive, recognising that all of us are wounded and the other person was acting out of their own inner wounds and unmet needs.

It is important, though, to take time to first process the pain of the experience; to weep, to scream, to let out any anger and to grieve what has happened. We must first face the hard reality of our feelings and process them safely. Only then, at the right time, might we be able to step back from the rawness of the pain and consider forgiving.

Forgiving someone is *not* something we do to make the other person feel better, but a choice that we make for our own wellbeing. It doesn't mean we excuse what happened. Or that it is forgotten. We can't go back and change what happened. We must now face it. When we can't forgive the other person, we become a prisoner of the hurt done to us. In forgiving, we are deciding to let go of the bad feelings we are holding in our heart about another person.

To forgive, then, is to choose to stop hurting ourselves and to free ourselves from feeling a victim. It is very much tied up with laying down the inner stories we tell ourselves; someone else may have hurt us deeply or some event may have shattered our life, but we are taking a decision to no longer waste energy ruminating about a situation in the past that we cannot change. Forgiveness is like spring-cleaning for our heart.

When forgiveness feels tough, it can almost feel as if we need to 'grit our teeth' and steel ourselves to do this hard thing. But Susan Atkinson describes the process of forgiving, very simply, as 'letting go of some of the hurts and burdens and painful memories we are carrying because of wrong done to us'.[58] Which is exactly what it is: a 'letting go'. It's not excusing what happened to us, it is something we do for our own mental wellbeing.

Many people misunderstand how forgiveness works. There is a misconception that it's only truly valid if the other person forgives you back and we all shake hands and live happily ever after. While that's neat and tidy, it may not happen like that. Sometimes the other person may show no remorse and have no desire to hear you say, 'I forgive you.' Worse still, they may react negatively to you telling them that. But that doesn't mean you can't forgive them. It's a heart thing. Karen Swartz puts it like this: 'Forgiveness is not just about saying the words. It is an active process in which you make a conscious decision to let go of negative feelings whether the person deserves it or not.'[59]

You cannot control what the other person will say, think or do. You can only control your own response. The crucial point is that as far as your healing is concerned, the receiving and giving of forgiveness is between you and God. No one else. It is a releasing of the pain of not forgiving; an active decision to not let your negative emotions consume you.

You may want to tell others that you forgive them, and to ask those whom you have hurt to forgive you. You need to be prepared for the possibility that they may or may not want to reciprocate your forgiveness. That's something you have no control over, and you have to let go of any expectations you have around that. What matters is that by forgiving them, you are freeing yourself from holding bitterness in your heart, with all the damage that can do to you.

As Archbishop Desmond Tutu writes, 'Whether it is the tormentor who tortured me brutally, the spouse who betrayed me, the boss who passed me over for a promotion, or the driver who cut me off during my morning commute, I face the same choice: to forgive or to seek revenge.'[60]

Forgiveness can be hard, but it leads to the beginnings of release from your pain.

Keiko Holmes

Unforgiveness imprisons you; tethers you to the perpetrator of your pain. Jesus said, 'I have come to set the prisoners free.'[61]

Keiko Holmes, founder of Agape World,[62] is a person whose ministry literally did that: set the prisoners free. After the Second World War, she painstakingly sought out men who had been Prisoners of War in the Far East. She befriended them and invited them to return to Japan with her on a pilgrimage of reconciliation.

This was real godly work. I know from my own uncle's story that those prisoners suffered terribly at the hands of the Japanese. They were starved, beaten and relentlessly tortured. My uncle carried the scars on his back for the whole of his life. But he carried even deeper scars in his heart, bearing a lifelong hatred for the Japanese nation.

I had the privilege of meeting Keiko, a slight little Japanese lady, a few years ago. She told me that when these former prisoners had the courage to return to Japan and meet the men who tortured them, that when they were able to look them in the eye and recognise their shared humanity, something remarkable often happened. An extraordinary bond often formed as the two, reunited, saw something of themselves in each other. Each had been just a young man at the time, dragged into a war they didn't want to be fighting, and obeying orders they didn't want to be carrying out. When the former Prisoner of War could get to the point where he could reach out his hand and say, 'I forgive you' to his former prison guard, the pain of years would fall away. Healing happened, not just in the heart but sometimes physically too.

If you search for them, you will be able to find many similar high-profile accounts of the healing power of forgiveness. There are also countless ordinary folk whose quiet forgiving never makes the headlines but who, in forgiving the inexcusable, have healed hearts and changed lives.

Forgiveness will help you to let go of your pain. It carries within it the seeds of hope and change.[63]

CHAPTER 8

Letting Go

*For everything there is a season,
a time for every activity under heaven.*
Ecclesiastes 3:1

Let it go.
It's not yours to carry.
Nathan Peterson [64]

A good declutter

I had a big sort out recently. It needed to happen. My garage was overflowing with mountains of stuff. I decided it was time for a few things to go. Out went boxes of files I had kept for twenty years. A large collection of plastic toys which grandsons had long since outgrown. Gardening tools which no longer saw the light of day. Assorted boxes which I thought would be useful one day. (They never were.) Half empty tins of paint, their contents now deteriorated. And so much more. All found new homes in charity shops or ended up at the rubbish tip. It was a relief when the task was done. The old had gone. There was space for the new. My whole heart felt lighter and freer.

It's not just garages and spare bedrooms but also lives that can be like that. When unwanted change surges through our life we often resist it, wanting to cling to who we were, to all that was familiar. I wonder if that's true of you. Are you wanting to cling to the identity you felt you had? Sometimes you need to let things go. The dream you had. The friendship you hoped would last forever. The way you thought life was going to be. The pay rise that never happened. The plan to walk the coastal path. The desire to spend more time with someone. As life changes, and it always does, you need to learn to let go. To let go and move on.

We let go continuously throughout our lifetime. We let go of our health as it begins to deteriorate. Of our favourite jumper when it becomes full of holes. If we are a parent, we let go of children as they fly the nest. We exchange the car which once served us well but now needs too much money spending on it. We let go. Change is the one constant in our life, a life full of many letting go moments.

As you emerge from your wounded place, there will be many things you need to let go of. You need to let go of any negative story you are telling yourself, and the strong emotions it stirs in you. You may have to let go of your view of how life was going to be, and the blame you may be placing on others. You need to gently let go of the tensions that have taken up residence in your body. There will be a whole gamut of things to let go of. They will be both unique to you and your situation and they will be important. But all of this will be part of freeing yourself from the pain and beginning to move on with life in a new way.

There is always a grief involved in letting something go, although not all losses carry the same weight. Your losses are not my losses, and your grief is not my grief, but that doesn't make it any less significant. Letting go can be hard. But sometimes it's life-giving. It frees up an energy for something new to emerge.

Symbolism can be very helpful in cementing this process; something you physically do to make the decision feel tangible. A couple of examples from my own story might help.

Lemon carnations

Lemon carnations were always his favourite, so I ordered a bunch; twenty-seven of them. One for each year of our marriage. The next day, the most painful day of my life, I snipped the heads off the flowers and took them with me in a little rucksack. Walking by the lake in a haze of grief, I knew that I had to prayerfully let go. I had to finally let go of all that had been and all that I always thought would be. I had to lay it down and move on.

My mind was anywhere but in that spot; my thoughts imagining two sons, side by side at their father's funeral. Without me. The grief was immense, the pain unbearable, the loneliness of the day crippling. I longed with all my heart to be shoulder to shoulder with the boys, supporting them through this day and feeling their strong arms holding me. But it was not to be.

I knew that the lake was the only place I wanted to be. It was my Stillness Spot; the place where I had found solace in the days of his dying. Dying, without me by his side. In the quietness of the morning, I was all alone. Alone with the water, the birds and my memories. And a box of lemon carnations. This was a day to say goodbye; a day to finally let go of all the pain that had hit me full force the day he walked out the door. Divorce was a heart-breaking severance. Being excluded from the funeral of the one whom I had done my best to love for half of my lifetime was unimaginably worse.

I sat down and simply gazed at the beauty of the scene. Everything seemed to have a crisp freshness, as if God had just that moment created it in all its perfection. Mallards made their way towards me, dragonflies hovered on bright yellow irises and a yellow-eyed duck dived for food. All was well with the world. Except that it wasn't.

I took in the scene with every ounce of my senses, breathed in the beauty, exhaled the pain, felt the weight of my emotions slide down. Then I knelt in the grass by the water's edge. Slowly, prayerfully, I gently cast each carnation on the water, giving thanks for each year of our life together. One; the year we began our life as a couple. Two; building a home for the future. Three; the joy when our first child was born. With each flower, a memory, a prayer, a thankfulness, a letting go. As twenty-seven lemon carnations drifted gently across the water, it was like a scattering of the ashes I would never get to hold. It was a release. It was a freedom. It was time to make a new start.

The helpfulness of symbolism

I didn't know it then, but there would be many other times when I would carry out similar rituals. Other times when the need to let go of a person or painful situation would draw me back to that healing place.

Letting go is important: whether it is people or pain, anger or worry, or words that echo in our heads. When the time is right, we need to let go if we are ever to become free of the pain of our past. To do something symbolic, where we let something slip through our fingers, or even aggressively throw it away, can be very helpful. I have done it many times. Always it has been healing. I have written words on balloons and stood and watched the breeze carry them high up into the sky until they were no more than a pinprick against the blue. I have prayed with stones, feeling the weight of the hurt and the loss, or the heaviness of a particular burden, then laid them at the foot of a cross, leaving them with Jesus. I have written out my angst in all its uncomfortable rawness, then watched it disintegrate in flames. I have learned to let go. Often. And always prayerfully.

A barbecue pit

A barbecue pit helped me to let go once. I had taken time out to process some pain. Unfortunately, the location was not quite as remote as I had hoped. My secluded log cabin proved to be directly under the path of the Red Arrows' training flights. Day after day I was treated to spectacular formations of the tiny red jets as the pilots honed their skills.

I was in a tough place emotionally, struggling with huge grief and angst. The pain was tearing me apart inside and I knew that I needed to let it go. I decided to write a letter; a letter that I never intended to send. I poured out all my disappointments and pain, all my anger and my grief. I let all that was brewing inside me spew out onto the paper. I held nothing back. Finally, it was done; all said. With a few heartfelt prayers I offered the pain to God, stepped outside and set fire to the letter in the barbecue pit. I watched the flames take hold, breathed in the smoke, watched the particles of ash dance in the air, and felt the catharsis of seeing it all disintegrate before my eyes.

The familiar jets roared overhead, but I paid no attention. I was fully in the moment, deeply invested in the heart-rending process of releasing my pain. Until it was done. Finally, as the embers died to white-grey ash and the last whispers of smoke curled upwards, I lifted my eyes to the sky and saw above me the most enormous red heart, traced in the sky by the signature smoke of the Red Arrows. It was as if it was painted in the sky just for me, as if God was saying, 'I love you.' In that moment I knew that I could move on from the pain.

Surrendering to peace

In each of the situations above, an extraordinary peace enveloped me when I had finally let go. Preparing myself to let go, however, was not like that. Not at all.

Remembering the detail of the pain, deciding how to symbolise its release, pouring all my angst out onto paper; all of that took immense internal energy and a painful revisiting of each situation, reliving every tension which had stirred in me.

It was the build-up to the symbolism that was hard, and it was exactly right that it should be. We need to completely feel the depth of our anger and grief before we can truly let it go.

But, having prayed beforehand and offered the future of all concerned to God, the actual letting go was peaceful. Peaceful and prayerful. The scattering of the flowers on the water and the placing of the paper into the flames; those actions were gentle and reverent. They were a peaceful surrender into a situation that I could do nothing to change. A release. An act of forgiveness. When it was over, there was a long slow exhale and a release of all the tensions which I'd held inside me for far too long. There was freedom. There was acceptance.

You too must let go when the time is right. At some stage, it's essential to let go of all the bitterness you may be holding on to. All the anger, the pain, the sadness, the despair. Whatever it is for you, for your own future wellbeing, you must let it go. Carrying all that pain long-term will become a burden that is too heavy to bear. Ask yourself, 'Is it helping me to carry this any longer?'

Acceptance

We can waste immense amounts of energy mentally fighting against how things are. In letting go, we cement our acceptance of where life has led us.

I've always been fascinated by Ordnance Survey maps. I love the fact that you can discern so much about the landscape without even setting foot outside the door. With modern technology there is far less reliance on printed maps today, but the ones I still find indispensable are the large billboard tourist maps often to be found in city centres. I easily get lost in a maze of unfamiliar streets, and it is always a relief to come across one of those large billboards and find the big arrow and those reassuring words, 'You are here.'

When I stand on a city street looking at a billboard map, the arrow clearly shows me that whether I wanted to be at this junction or not, it is, in fact, where I am. I am 'here'. And this is the only place from where I can move on. In your place of suffering, usually you don't want to be 'where you are'. But there is no other place to be. It's your reality. It's the place life has brought you to. And accepting that, rather than fighting it or denying it, is an important step in beginning to pick yourself up and move forward. As Henri Nouwen observes, 'The issue is not where you are but how you live wherever you are.'[65]

I once had the privilege of leading a meditation at the funeral of a friend. In the final days of her life, she asked me if I would write and lead a reflection entitled, 'In acceptance lies peace'. Those words have stayed with me ever since and they mirrored what I saw in

Chris as she lived her life and as she approached her death. When we can't accept the way things are, when we wrestle with the situation and fight against it, it takes so much energy. Resisting the situation depletes us mentally and physically, and spiritually too. It makes an already difficult situation many times harder. We function best when we can accept how life is right now.

In acceptance lies peace.

Pause Point

Where I am

Settle yourself into stillness with one of the breathing exercises. Then invite God to be with you.

Pick up a notebook and pen and write down what it is that you must accept.

Start with the words, 'This is where I am:', and end with the words, 'I will no longer fight against this reality but will accept that this is how it is. I choose to heal from this and move forward.'

Ask God to help you to accept your situation and begin that moving forward.

Make a list of what you need to let go of.

CHAPTER 9

Actively Forgiving

Forgiveness is nothing less than
the way we heal the world.
Archbishop Desmond Tutu[66]

Forgive us our sins,
as we forgive those who sin against us.
Luke 11:4

The intertwining

Forgiveness and symbolically letting go are inextricably intertwined. Choosing to forgive is a letting go of the bitterness you feel towards another, and a freeing yourself from the pain of holding on to that emotion, with its effects upon your mind and your health. When it is thoughts that we are letting go of, incorporating symbolism helps with a tangible cementing of that forgiveness, a completion of the process. When taken together, this decision and this action mark an important acceptance of your current situation. Once you have reached that point of acceptance, the entire energy of your circumstances will begin to change. From that point on, you will be able to face your situation in a more positive way, rather than ruminating on what cannot now be changed and living with a downcast negative viewpoint. It will mark a pivotal point in your journey towards the future.

Forgiveness is tied in with acceptance. Until we accept our difficult and unchosen circumstances we are internally fighting against the situation, often laying the blame at someone else's door. Only when we acknowledge that others in our story are struggling in their own way can we forgive and accept. Only then can we say:

> This is where I now am.
> I let go of the fact that your words and actions have wounded me.
> I choose to forgive you, and I will find a new way to move forward from this.

Steps in the forgiveness process

Carrying churning thoughts of bitterness towards others has a seriously damaging impact on our health and disrupts the possibility of finding inner peace. And the same is true of any burden of shame or guilt which we may be shouldering. The choice to lay these thoughts down and let them go is entirely in our own hands.

Once you have decided that you want to let go of these burdens it is well worth spending a little time preparing for that moment. The following questions are worth considering:

- What do I want God to *forgive me* for?
- What do I want to *forgive others* for?
- With *what symbolism* will I mark this process?
- *When, where* and *with whom* will I do this?

Getting clarity

Only you will know who and what you want to forgive or be forgiven for. In terms of forgiving other people, the answers might immediately come to mind for you; it will be the people and behaviours that have angered, saddened, or deeply hurt you. It can be harder with our own wrongdoings. Sometimes we have to search our conscience or take a deep dive into our memories in order to acknowledge the things we have done wrong, or less well than we could have; the things we're ashamed of, or have a sense of guilt about. This can be a painful process but one which is well worth going through.

Have a sacred moment and spend some time reflecting on all the things that you want to ask God to forgive you for. I remember clearly that the first time I ever did this I came up with a massive list. It's perfectly OK if that's how it is for you. Get it all out. Take time to let all your regrets surface. Then think about all the people whose actions or words, or maybe lack of actions, you want to forgive. Make a list of those things too if it helps.

Pause Point

Getting clarity

Stage 1:

Bring yourself to stillness in your preferred way.

Say a simple prayer and ask God to help you.

Let your mind gently play through your memories and just be still with the question, 'What words, thoughts or behaviours of mine am I ashamed about or regret?'

Ask the Holy Spirit to bring those things to mind.

Just sit with the question and let the answers pop into your head. Make a note of those answers.

Stage 2:

When you are ready, turn your attention to other people.

Now, think about those whom you want to forgive; those who have hurt you, made you angry, disappointed you, or caused you sadness.

Be aware of exactly who and what you are making a choice to forgive.

Don't rush this bit. And don't go down a rabbit hole of emotion. Just let the answer simply rise to the surface of your mind.

Pause for as long as you need to.

Make a 'heart decision' to choose to forgive, no matter how hard it feels.

With Jesus' help, you can do this.

Choosing a letting-go symbolism

Your forgiveness needs to be sealed with an action. Combining forgiveness with a symbolic letting go is powerful and freeing. It is the combination of prayer, symbolism and intentionality that makes it so. It can set you free from burdensome thoughts and change how you feel in both your mind and your body. It can be a significant step in your return to wellbeing.

When I scattered those lemon flowerheads on the lake, I did several other things as well. I began by recalling and saying sorry for all the mistakes I had made, all the things I had done wrong and all my failures to love, and I prayerfully asked God to forgive me each one. With each 'sorry', I held a stone, felt the weight of that failure, and then dropped the stone into the water. I let that memory go.

A little further round the lake, I scattered the flowers on the water, praying with each one first. Finally, on the far shore, I released two helium-filled balloons; one to totally let go of all that had been, and one to embrace whatever was yet to come. As they climbed higher and higher into the blue, I felt myself drawing a line under all that had been so painful. As I set the balloons free, they in turn set me free.

Once you have reached the point of feeling able to do so, saying to God that you forgive someone can be as simple as that; just voicing it in prayer. But sealing that forgiveness in your heart is less easy. That is why using some tactile symbolism, physically letting go of something, can be very helpful. There is something about the physicality of that action that roots itself in your consciousness. You have done it. You have forgiven, and you have let it go. When and if you look back, as you surely will, it is the plop of the stones in the water, or the drifting away of the flowerheads you will remember, and your heart will remind you, 'I have let it go.'

Decide in advance what your chosen 'letting go' symbolism will be. You could smash a pot to represent the brokenness you feel, and pray with each broken piece. You could write out all your grievances and then put the paper through a shredder, or (safely) set fire to it. Perhaps you might like to use flowerheads floating away on water, as I did, or little paper boats with words or pictures on them. I know people who have hammered nails into wood, written words on balloons and released them, chalked their grievances on a slate and then wiped the slate clean. Or you could use stones, feeling the weight of the pain as you let each one go. Only you will know what feels right for you. It's your choice. Be creative. Decide on what will feel most meaningful for you, and gather the materials you need.

When, where and with whom

Think carefully about whether you will do your prayerful forgiveness alone, or whether there is someone you would like to ask to be alongside you. In some church traditions people choose to do this with a priest, but it's certainly not essential.

Decide also when and where you will do this. If you choose to do it outside, where will you go? If indoors, prepare the space in some way; maybe light a candle, if you have one. Whatever works for you. Remember to switch off any distractive technology that might beep at you. The more thought you put into this, the more meaningful, healing and long-lasting the exercise will be for you.

Just do it

A primary school version of the Lord's Prayer translates the more familiar words about forgiveness as, 'Help us when we are wrong and clean us up on the inside. Help us to let other people off and move on.'[67]

Remember that though you might want to voice or write your forgiveness to the other person, this is not initially about that. This is a healing conversation between you and Jesus or, if you prefer, between you and God. It involves two things. You are asking God to forgive you. And you are saying to God that you forgive the other person. You are choosing to stop holding on to the bitterness that is damaging you and contributing to you feeling unwell. This process is, initially, purely for you: to help you to let go and begin to move on.

Having prepared the ground and decided how you will mark your act of forgiveness, all that remains now is for you to do it. You may want to carry it out in two stages (firstly, seeking God's forgiveness for yourself, and secondly, voicing forgiveness for others), or you may decide to do both at the same time.

In your chosen place, and with your symbolism to hand, first calm yourself in your preferred way. Breathe slowly, take in your surroundings with all your senses and become aware that God is with you (even if you cannot tangibly feel his presence). Now simply begin to pray. Start by asking God to help you. Then, in your own words, talk to him first about all your own failures and wrongdoings and ask him to forgive you.

After you have voiced those things prayerfully, just be still for a while, breathe slowly and know that his forgiveness is flooding over you. Allow yourself to feel it and receive it. Let go symbolically of each painful thing you have brought to God, preferably saying out loud, 'Thank you, God. I now receive your forgiveness and let this go.'

Move on then to talk to God about those people and situations which you are actively choosing to forgive. With each act of forgiveness, take time to recall the pain you feel about it before you speak the words. As you speak the words, 'I choose to forgive *(person)* for *(the action)*', perform your symbolic letting go. Take your time over each statement of forgiveness. Don't rush. Feel the depth and the importance of what you are doing.

Finally, rest in the stillness. Prayerfully say thank you to God. And feel the weight of all the difficult thoughts you have carried simply falling away. Take some slow, deep breaths and let the peace of God fill you.

Afterword

Walk away from that prayer time knowing that the slate is wiped clean: you have said that you are sorry, and you have been forgiven. And you have forgiven in your heart, in the presence of God, those who have wronged and hurt you. Step outside, if you are not already there, and take some deep breaths of fresh air. Notice yourself relaxing. Be fully aware of your bodily tensions softening. Breathe in deep draughts of peace. Be fully in the moment. Feel the freedom of not having to worry any more about the things you have just prayed about.

After that, simply let them go. Let go as totally as children do. When my grandsons were little, having said sorry for their behaviour, when their father had given them a hug or a 'high five', they would go straight back to playing with their toys. They knew what they had done was naughty, but they also knew they had been forgiven. It was over. They moved on. You can do the same.

Your old thoughts about those situations will inevitably pop back into your head from time to time. Learn to just be aware of them and then let them go, reminding yourself that they have been forgiven. When one of his disciples asked Jesus if he should forgive someone as many as seven times, Jesus' reply was 'No, not seven times, but seventy times seven!'[68] In other words, we must keep on forgiving; just as God's love is without limit, our forgiveness should be without limit.

The clean slate

The image of a slate being wiped clean is a lovely one to describe what happens when we forgive or are forgiven. From the very moment we begin to say sorry to God, we are forgiven. Totally. Completely. Instantaneously. We can let go of that concern and make a new start. The slate is clean. The result of forgiveness is described that way in *The Message* version of the Bible:

> Count yourself lucky,
> how happy you must be – you get a fresh start,
> your slate's wiped clean.
> *Psalm 32:1, MSG*

I doubt if there are any places where this happens now, but in my father's lifetime it used to be commonplace to ask a shopkeeper or a barmaid to 'put it on the slate'. It was a request to have some credit for goods you couldn't pay for on that day, and the slate chalkboard sat on the counter as a reminder to everyone that this bill still had to be paid. My dad often used to have a couple of pints of beer 'on the slate' and then settle his debt when he got his weekly pay packet.

But here's the great thing about Jesus: your 'slate' with God is now completely clean. Jesus has wiped it clean for you. So, when those little niggling reminders of the things you have been forgiven for keep trying to make a comeback, just remember that the slate is clean. It's a done deal.

I sometimes carry a small piece of slate in my pocket to remind myself of that. If you have a neighbour with slate chippings on their drive or in their garden, you might like to beg a piece from them and do the same. You don't need to tell them why you'd like it. Hold on to your piece of slate. Finger it in your pocket. Or look at it often on your windowsill, or wherever else you decide to keep it.

Remember: the slate is clean.

Let it all go.

Make a new start.

CHAPTER 10

The Problem of Worry

Give all your worries and cares to God,
for he cares about you.
1 Peter 5:7

All shall be well, and all manner
of things shall be well.
Julian of Norwich[69]

Living the Jesus way

Within these pages, we have explored how current scientific understandings of the workings of the mind and body relate to the paraphrased instructions of Jesus with which we began:

Don't worry. Don't be afraid.
Don't be angry. Forgive often.
Let go of your burdens. Be thankful.
Be still. Rest. Pray.

The more we learn how to live out those instructions, the more we realise how essential they are to our own health and wellbeing. And among them, the pivotal one is practising forgiveness. As often as it is needed. 'Seventy times seven' times[70] if necessary. Forgiveness is absolutely, 100 per cent, key to our healing; both knowing ourselves forgiven and forgiving others. And it's one of the gifts of Jesus. He came to set the captives free.[71]

It can be desperately hard to forgive but it is truly life-giving. It is even harder, though, to live a life crippled by bitterness and anger, or to be trapped in the self-hatred of guilt and shame. The question of whether someone else in our life deserves our forgiveness is totally irrelevant. Forgiveness helps us to let go of the inner rage which is doing nothing but harm us. It sets us free from the thoughts which are otherwise keeping us trapped in a cycle of turmoil and suffering.

But it's a choice. As is acceptance. We are where we are. The past cannot be changed and there is nothing to be gained by internally wrestling against where our circumstances have brought us. We cannot rewind life. The only healthy way to progress is to draw a line under everything and move forward.

The problem of worry

Forgiveness, letting go, understanding that all of us are wounded; all these things can help us to go far on our journey into healing. But there is still the thorny issue of how to calm our fears and anxieties. We now understand that all our fears originate from the brain's sophisticated alert system. We have also learned that this 'fear warning system' fires up our body to take protective physical action and that's what gives rise to the strange bodily sensations that accompany our fears. So, we now have some understanding of how our fears kick in and why our bodies feel so disturbed by them. That knowledge is good and helpful, but fears still pop up, even when the underlying cause of them is far from life-threatening.

True fear is the brain's automatic reaction when it wants to get our attention about something that is a danger to us. It's entirely involuntarily. It just arises, instantly. Worry is a different form of fear. Worry is a thought-generated anxiety about a situation that doesn't currently exist, but which may happen in the future. And it is often an anxiety that lingers. Worries are of our own making. They are a product of our imagination in its 'worst case scenario' mode. Our mind is imagining something bad which might happen and then reacting, not to how things are right now, but to our imagined picture of the future event.

If we can be accepting of what life brings to our door and at peace with whatever might happen tomorrow, or at any other point in the future, then that is true inner healing. And it's a very happy and peaceful place to be. But how do we achieve that state of heart and mind? Having accepted where we are, identified and let go of unhelpful inner narratives and forgiven those who have wounded us, the thing that now stands in the way of us being at peace is our worries. Jesus had some wisdom about this. He said, 'Don't worry about tomorrow'.[72] But we so often do. And while we worry, we are never fully at peace.

Love changes everything

How do we silence those worries? The answer to that question lies in understanding who God is, and who we are in relation to God. The life of Jesus, as told in Scripture, gives us a true insight into the heart of God, because Jesus was the embodiment of God. And what we see is love; pure, unadulterated love. A love that reaches out and heals, without judgement. No questions asked. No holds barred. No one excluded. The Bible states it emphatically: 'God is love.'[73] The internationally respected psychologist David Benner sums it up beautifully when he writes, 'Regardless of what you have come to believe about God based on your life experience, the truth is that when God thinks of you, love swells in his heart and a smile comes to his face. God bursts with love for humans.'[74]

To know ourselves loved is the most healing thing in the world. Mother Teresa acknowledged that when she said, 'The hunger for love is much more difficult to remove than the hunger for bread.'[75] Love can heal even the deepest wounds, the most fractured relationships, the most battered lives. But I do understand that those are hard words to read if your experience has been one of rejection or abuse. It can be very difficult to believe God cares about you if lots of painful things have happened in your life. This is especially true if you have been neglected or ill-treated and haven't experienced love from other human beings, either in your childhood or in later years. You may well be angry that I even dare to suggest that God loves you.

But he does. His love pulses through the universe. Whether or not you believe in God, God believes in you. And his love is of another dimension; it is far greater than any other human being could ever bless you with. That suggestion may take a bit of a leap of trust on your part, but it's true. You may feel yourself to be unlovable. But believe me, you're not. Not at all. Not in God's eyes.

Prodigal welcome

The Bible story of the prodigal son[76] is a wonderful illustration of the magnitude of God's love for us. A son begged his father for his inheritance, then went away and squandered it on wild living until he was reduced to the point of feeding pigs, while all the time going hungry himself. He made a real mess of his life and didn't expect his father to ever be able to forgive him. Destitute and desperate, he returned home to beg his father to take him on simply as a hired hand. Contrary to all his expectations, his father, who had been looking out for him all the time, not only forgave him but actively raced to meet him, flung his arms around him and threw a party.

No matter how messed up our life might feel, God is constantly longing for us to turn to him. And when we do, we'll find him racing towards us to welcome us 'home', with a love that's greater than we can begin to imagine. No mistakes are irredeemable. 'Nothing ... can separate us from God's love'.[77] Absolutely nothing. We simply need to be open to receive it. And that takes trust.

Trusting in God's care

Fears can dissipate once you know, once you really know, that you are held and loved by Someone much greater than yourself. Held and loved by the Creator of the universe. But that can be hard to believe when you are feeling at your most unlovable. Sometimes a visual interpretation can help. Author and artist Charlie Mackesy has created many beautifully moving sculptures[78] and paintings[79] of this story; the father embracing the prodigal son. His powerful imagery takes the viewer beyond the words of scripture to an almost visceral sensation of how life-changing such all-embracing love can be. At their heart, Mackesy's artworks are all images of someone having a strong and deeply loving hug.

When a toddler is afraid, having a parent wrap their arms around them and speak words of love to them reassures them they are safe. They no longer fear. They are safe in the arms of someone who loves them and will care for them in the way that they know is best for them. Which is what God promises us: 'I know the plans I have for you. . . . They are plans for good and not for disaster, to give you a future and a hope.'[80] Your fears can subside when you dare to believe that you have God's perfect love on your side. Remember the words on that narrowboat? *Love over fear.*

Daring to trust

Love and trust go hand in hand. When you know that a person loves you, really loves you, it is entirely natural to trust them. As you grow deeper into a relationship with God, as you begin to see and hear of answers to prayer, your level of trust in his promises will grow. He tells us: 'Don't be afraid, for I am with you. . . . I will strengthen you and help you.'[81] For now, I simply invite you to dare to take the risk of trusting. Letting go of our worries becomes possible when we trust that we are placing them in the hands of a loving God who has ultimate control and who only and always has our best interests at heart. And he invites us to do just that: 'Give all your worries and cares to God, for he cares about you.'[82]

Clearly, it is important to think things through and to prepare wisely for possible problematic situations. But having registered the fact that we are concerned, if there is no helpful action we can take, then persisting with the worry will serve no good purpose. As Mark Twain is reputed to have said, 'I've had lots of worries in my life, most of which never happened.'[83]

We rarely have just one concern. Often, we have a whole cacophony of worries rattling round in our heads, bouncing around in there and deepening and getting more and more knotted up together as they collide. When all our worries get entangled together, the overall weight of them can sometimes feel overwhelming. It can be helpful to intentionally take time to carefully unravel them and look at each worry in isolation from the others. The following is a simple practice that can help with this.

Pause Point

Examining your worries

Stage 1: Naming your worries:

With your notebook to hand, bring yourself to a place of quiet stillness.

Invite God into this time of reflection.

Let your mind be still as you sit with the question, 'What am I worried about?'

Ask the Holy Spirit to bring each anxiety to mind, one at a time.

With each worry that surfaces, simply write it down in your notebook, then return to the quiet and let your mind identify the next concern.

Repeat this process as often as you need to, until you have every single worry written down.

Take a short pause before moving to the next step.

Stage 2: Examining your list:

With each worry on your list, ask yourself the question, 'Can I do anything about this, or is the outcome of the situation I am worrying about totally outside my control?'

If you personally can do nothing to change what might happen, draw a line through that worry in your notebook.

Repeat this until you have considered every worry.

Stage 3: Letting go:

At the end of this process, you will have realised which worries you can do something about and which you can't. There is no point in giving headspace to things you cannot control, so with each worry that you have drawn a line through, decide now to cease worrying about it. And prayerfully hand over the problem to God. You might find it helpful to include some symbolism in that letting go.

Stage 4: Making a plan:

Now look at the shorter list of concerns; those which you might be able to do at least one small thing towards resolving. For each of those worries, take time to decide what helpful action you can take next. Write those actions down in your notebook. Prioritise them and activate them one at a time when you feel strong enough.

When anxieties crop up in the future, deal with each one in the same way, before they have chance to spiral out of control. Every time a worry pops up, examine it objectively. If what you imagine might happen is beyond your control, let it go. Hand it over to God. God knows every detail of your situation and he knows the plans he has for you. And his plans are always good. Let each worry go. Trust that God is in control.

Triggers

There will be times when something unexpected throws you right back to the state of mind you felt you had recovered from. It might be a significant life event. Or it could be as simple as a snippet of a song, a familiar fragrance, or a phrase in a book. This is completely normal. Life keeps happening, in ways over which we have no control, and our sophisticated brain makes connections to pain in the past that still lingers within us. Grief, in particular, has an untidy dynamic and can return in powerful waves long after the initial loss.

Don't fight it if one day you're plummeted back into pain and tough emotions. Your reaction is simply an indication that there's a little more healing to be done; a deeper layer of earlier pain that still has a residue within you. Take space. Take stock. Return to the lessons in this book and you will quickly emerge again. You will be able to recover your peace.

CHAPTER 11

The Power of the Pause

Be still before the LORD and wait patiently for him.
Psalm 37:7, NIV

Let the peace of Christ rule in your hearts . . .
Colossians 3:15, NIV

Holistic wellbeing

So, what do I mean by inner healing? And, having begun this journey with me, how might you deepen and sustain that healing?

I wonder what you were seeking when you first delved inside the covers of this book? Relief from depression? Freedom from anxiety? Calmness in your struggles? Clarity in the chaos? Hope for happier times? Maybe something you couldn't give voice to but somehow knew you needed?

Healing is all those things and more.

In its broadest sense, inner healing is freedom from all those emotions which hold us back from being peaceful and happy. Freedom from shame, anxiety and hatred. Freedom from anger, bitterness and all the other crippling emotions we've been facing together throughout this book. Tim Stead defines it as 'the process by which we become as whole and as free as it's possible for each of us to be as human beings'.[84] And we become more whole when we learn to integrate our lived experiences peacefully, not painfully. At its very best, inner healing is a very holistic sense of wellbeing, which can be sustained regardless of our circumstances. It is a feeling of being at peace with yourself, at peace with others and at peace with the world, whatever life throws at you.

Let me say that again:

> True inner healing is being at peace with yourself, at peace with others and at peace with the world, whatever life throws at you.

That's a big ask, I know. The Hebrew word for this is *shalom*, which can be understood to mean a state of peace, harmony and wholeness. Few of us feel that sense of harmony all the time, but it is possible to experience it often and to learn to grow more fully into it. It doesn't mean the complete absence of illness or struggle, but rather an awareness of being at peace within your situation.

A healing God

The Bible proclaims that God is a healing God. In the very first definition of himself in the Bible, God says,

'I am the LORD who heals you.'[85] God's whole essence is love and his very nature is to heal us. We are hardwired to be in relationship with him. And the only way to cultivate an unshakeable depth of *shalom* is to learn to grow closer to God. Without that closeness to our Maker, we are not fully whole. It is in our day-to-day relationship with God that our healing becomes sustained. It is the work of a lifetime, but it can begin today.

Whether you've been a Christian for years or whether you've only just cautiously dipped your toe into the waters of prayer, you may still be wondering how you can 'know' God's presence with you. It's hard to explain, but sometimes it just happens. Sometimes you just know. Often God breaks through to us in the darkest of times, in the lowest points of our lives. On my own recovery from breakdown, I discovered many understandings and practices which helped me to heal. I have shared the most significant ones in this book. What I also discovered, though, and what was completely outside my comfort zone at the time, was a relationship with God.

The shaft of sunlight

There was a defining moment for me in a quiet chapel. Such awakenings can happen anywhere, at any time, but that was where it was for me. I can still see the little puddles of tears on the stone floor by my sandals, feel the exhaustion that followed when the tears were spent, and then the tangible, totally unexpected sense of being 'held' in a deep, warm silence. There were no words. I was totally alone in the silence of the chapel. And yet I knew, in a way that one can never subsequently unknow, that I was not alone. That was my first experience of the invisible power and presence of the Divine. Of God. Of God being closer than a whisper.

Nothing was magically or instantaneously made better. I still felt in a black hole of pain. Elements of suffering still wrestled within me. But something had changed. Something had changed big-style. It was as if a shaft of sunlight had pierced the impenetrable darkness, somehow enabling me to step back and be aware of a bigger picture that was mysteriously held in love and intrinsic goodness. My pain was not the dominant all-consuming reality that it had previously seemed. There were other perspectives. And that gave me hope. Something within my mental landscape had shifted. In my darkness, there was suddenly an indefinable glimmer of light that refused to be extinguished.

The danger of sharing my story, of course, is that I run the risk of you feeling that any sense that you have had, or not had, of God's presence is somehow diminished because your experience has been different. I share this merely to explain how my own inner healing began to unfold. There were many other elements to it, but the silence was an important catalyst. I didn't seek out or expect to have the experience, but it happened.

Your circumstances will be different. As will your journey. Any 'felt sense', or otherwise, that you have of God will be different. But the key thing I want to share is that silence can help. It can be the beginnings of prayer, and it can help you to heal. Paraphrasing the title of a book by Stephen Cottrell – doing nothing can really change your life.[86]

The power of prayer

After I became aware of that 'presence' in the silence, I began to pray. Over time, I came to understand, as Sharon Garlough Brown says, that: 'Prayer is about being deeply loved.'[87] It's only when you begin to trust how deeply God loves you that prayer begins to make any sense. God loves you. Really loves you. He will never harm you, reject you, or ignore you. He will always respond in the way he knows is best for you. That is the heart of why it makes sense to pray, and why it makes no sense not to.

We should never underestimate the power of prayer. At the height of his medical profession, pioneering surgeon and Nobel Prize winner, Alexis Carrel, spoke of it as being the most powerful form of energy one can generate,[88] and claimed that the effects of prayer on the human body are as demonstrable as are other biological processes.[89] Prayer is powerful.

The more we get to know God's presence with us and to learn about his character, the greater confidence we will have in his promises. And there are many ways to be drawn into that God-centred reality. We can deepen our knowledge of God through studying Scripture and learning from other Christians. And all those things are good. But there is no substitute for prayer.

There are a multitude of ways to pray. The more you pray, the more you will deepen your relationship with God and the more you will begin to recognise him at work in your life. Talking to God, either verbally or in the silence of your thoughts, is the way most of us tentatively start. Praying together with others can give added strength to our prayers, and asking others to pray for us is an excellent thing to do. Occasionally one simple prayer can bring about remarkable healing.

The Bible encourages us, in fact, to pray constantly. 'Never stop praying',[90] we read in Scripture. This is easier than you might think. It isn't about sitting down continually with a candle before you and a Bible in your hand, but more about taking every thought that pops into your head and simply lifting it up to God in prayer. You can do this wherever you are and whatever you are doing. When you are waiting at the supermarket checkout, walking down the street, washing up at the sink; every moment can become a prayer. Every incident or challenging thought can become a holy moment. With every thought that pops into your head, just deflect it to God with a prayer: 'Lord, I place this in your hands. Please bless this situation (or person).' It easily becomes a habit and it's powerful. Incorporating prayer into all the moments of your days in this way helps you to let go of worry, blesses others and builds a greater intimacy with God.

Prayerfully imagining yourself inside a Bible story can also be a very powerful way to pray. If you have ever 'got lost' inside a good novel, you will know how easy and natural it is to imagine yourself inside the story.

Without really trying, you find yourself immersed in the detail, picturing the scene, feeling the emotions of the characters, being there in vivid detail. Reading the Bible can be just the same but with an added extra; in reading Scripture, you can have a close encounter with Jesus. And Jesus is the healer par-excellence.

There are many accounts in the Bible of Jesus healing people and, as Russ Parker, former director of Acorn Christian Healing Foundation,[91] writes, 'Anything which helps us discern and practise the presence of Jesus will become for us a channel of healing.'[92] Imaginative contemplation is a prayer exercise that I often use when leading healing retreats and it is can be very effective. Prayerfully immersing yourself inside the story, noticing the details with all your senses and coming face to face with Jesus through your imagination can be powerfully healing.

Simply read the story slowly, a couple of times. As you read, picture yourself in the scene, using every ounce of your senses. Where are you in the story? What can you see and hear and smell? Let your mind wander through the scene in your imagination, noticing what happens at every stage and being aware of what feelings surface in you. Feel yourself inside the story. And as the story develops, begin to talk to Jesus about what is emerging for you. And notice especially how Jesus responds to you.

For more resources on prayer, and for examples of healing scriptures to pray imaginatively with, see Appendices 1 and 2.

Silence and stillness

Prayer is like oxygen for the soul. The more you pray, the more you will begin to see positive changes within you and around you. And the more that happens, the easier and more natural it will become to have a deeper trust in God's work in your life. And that will lead you to want to pray more. Any form of prayer can help in your search for healing. But listening to, or simply just 'being' with God, is equally vital.

In my own experience, the presence of God is often most deeply encountered in intentional silence. God himself invites us to spend time in that way. We read in the Psalms, 'Be still, and know that I am God!'[93] That is why I have gently introduced the practice of silence and stillness throughout this book. It may not happen immediately, but as you become more comfortable with sitting with God in silence, you may begin to know his presence with you more deeply. You might sometimes sense a tangible feeling of love enfolding and holding you in the silence. In other words, you may find yourself *experiencing* God, rather than simply *knowing about* him, and this can become a turning point in your confidence and trust in the reality of his love for you. And with a growing level of trust, it will be easier to hand your worries over to God, and let them go, knowing that he only and always wants the best for you. Indeed, the Bible tells us, 'In quietness and trust is your strength'.[94]

When we totally trust that God really is on our side and is in control of events ultimately working out in the best possible way, then it becomes easier to hand over every concern to him. He sees the bigger picture. He knows better than we do how to bring new life out of tough situations. He is, after all, a resurrection God. And he 'causes everything to work together for the good of those who love [him]'.[95]

It takes time to develop trust in other people whom we engage with. It grows as we spend time with them, and as we get to know more about their character and behaviour. Trust develops as we experience their love in action. Developing trust in God's protection is no different. The more we hang out with God and observe what he does, the more our confidence in his care will grow. And punctuating our days with times of silence, with 'pause points', helps to enable that. Intentionally spending time with God, just 'being', is the essence of prayer.

The power of the pause

The power of taking a pause has been introduced throughout this book and will be pivotal in your ongoing future wellbeing. It is an often overlooked, simple tool, in maintaining good health. Countless practitioners of mindfulness and meditation enjoy the regular benefits of this practice. It costs nothing, needs no special equipment, has no bad side effects and anyone can do it. And it's inherently Christian too. Jesus frequently withdrew to quiet places, to rest and to pray.[96] The present moment, this exact 'now', holds great power when we are open to being still within it. It has the potential to lead us to a quiet peace beneath the hamster wheel of our whirling thoughts and to give us insights into what will be most helpful for us.

In my slow recovery from breakdown, a turning point came for me when I began to embrace regular stillness. Regular pauses when I intentionally set aside time each day to just 'be'. To be quiet. To try to let go of all the thoughts that were constantly fighting each other in my head. Times when I stopped the never-ending battle of trying to make sense of it all, of trying to find a way through on my own. The more I allowed negative thoughts to rage, the more the pain intensified and the harder the battle became. Stillness helped me to still those thoughts.

Whatever our life circumstances, we all need to give ourselves permission to take space, both physically and, more importantly, mentally. When we are feeling overwhelmed, nothing is more important. We are constantly surrounded by noise and visual stimulation. And in the overconnected digital world that we now inhabit, it has become the norm to be instantly connected and always available. When did you last unplug? Human beings are not designed to be 'always on'. The pause moments are like pit stops in our often frenetically busy lives. They are opportunities to take our foot off the pedal, however briefly, and take time to rest, recharge and refuel. They are critical.

Our minds need solitude, stillness and silence just as much as our bodies need physical rest. It's only in becoming still, in both mind and body, that we can begin to hear the whispers of our soul. Only in those moments, when we stop long enough to truly take a long, lingering look at our inner world, can we become aware of and begin to face how we are really feeling. And that is the beginning of healing. Quiet pauses can calm us, allow our swirling thoughts to settle, and bring a clarity that is missing when we don't allow ourselves to pay attention to our inner reality. They can draw our mind back from its preoccupations about the past or its anxieties about the future, returning us to the 'now'. They become a safe space for deep pain and grief to be tended. And more importantly, they can become holy encounters. They help us to be present to the God who is always present with us but often unnoticed. Our 'pause points' are a form of prayer. And they can be life-changing.

As I have developed my knowledge of healing over the years, I have come to the inescapable conclusion that a relationship with God, through Jesus, is foundational to true and lasting healing. Fear of one sort or another underpins all our painful emotions. It is only through the never-ending source of love that exists beyond our self that we will be able to calm absolutely every fear and find a depth of peace that is beyond explanation. The love of God is perhaps the only thing that makes that possible in every circumstance. My prayer is that you will come to know the healing nature of that love in your own life. It deepens through the 'pause points'. Take time to be still and quiet. Often. It will help. Inner stillness develops inner peace. And that is healing.

As you develop your capacity for inner stillness, you will find that you create a reservoir of peace within yourself that you can draw upon amid any external chaos or struggle that may surround you. Then you might one day be able to say, as a wise friend of mine often does, 'As long as I'm alright on the inside, everything's alright on the outside, even when it's not.' That is true healing; being so rooted in a trust that God will care for you that you can be at peace, moment by moment, whatever happens. That's the unshakeable peace that Jesus wants to develop in you. It's the peace that he spoke of when he said, 'I am leaving you with a gift – peace of mind and heart.'[97]

I pray that you will come to know that gift of peace. It can begin to happen when you promise yourself that you will weave regular moments of quiet stillness into your life. And even if you have absolutely no sense of God with you in those times, it doesn't matter. He will be there, hidden but present. And the regular times of quiet stillness will have huge benefits for your health and wellbeing.

CHAPTER 12

One Step at a Time

A journey of a thousand miles
begins with a single step.
Lao Tzu[98]

'For I know the plans I have for you,' says the LORD.
'They are plans for good and not for disaster,
to give you a future and a hope.'
Jeremiah 29:11

Swedish arrows and Japanese pottery

It's no secret that I am not a fan of tattoos. Nevertheless, my son has several and there is one that lifts my spirits every time I see it. It's a depiction of a Malin arrow: a Swedish symbol that features an infinity sign with an arrow going through it. Not only is it attractive, but the combination of the arrow and the infinity symbol is extremely powerful. It represents the fact that setbacks in life are inevitable, but that doesn't mean that you can't grow from them and keep moving forwards in positive ways. An arrow, after all, must always be drawn backwards in the bow to generate the power for it to fly. Whenever we hit a patch in life where we feel 'held back', there is always the potential to find new energy for positive transformation.

Any tattoo inevitably has a story behind it. The Malin arrow is a very positive piece of artwork. I'm proud of my son for having chosen to have it inked on his forearm, because I'm thrilled at what it says about his character. The path through life is never a straight line. It may be completely different to what we thought it would be, but that doesn't mean it can't be infinitely good. Every choice we make can lead us to a better place.

Times of feeling broken are inevitable. Most of us find ourselves in such a place at least once in our lives. All of us become wounded in one way or another. But as Patrick Regan, of Kintsugi Hope[99] writes, 'We shouldn't be ashamed of our scars, because a scar is always a place of healing.'[100] The organisation that he founded is a charity that strives to make a difference to people's mental health. The charity takes its name from the Japanese principle of 'Kintsugi', which is a technique for repairing pottery with seams of gold. The word means 'golden joinery' in Japanese. Instead of hiding the scars, the practitioners of Kintsugi make a feature of them. They repair the brokenness in a way that makes the object more beautiful, and even more unique than it was prior to being broken. I love this concept, not only because it makes beautiful pottery, but because it reminds me that being open about my wounds can be the first important step towards healing them and integrating them into a brighter, more beautiful future.

Sheridan Voysey, writing about starting again after a dream has died, writes, 'Perhaps a greater tragedy than a broken dream is a life forever defined by it.'[101]

Wounds, once healed, have the capacity to change our perspective on life in very positive ways. Gathering wounds along life's complicated journey is part and parcel of becoming the utterly unique human being that we are. 'Can beauty ever come from this sense of brokenness?' you may ask. Yes, it can. Some of the most peaceful and compassionate people I know are those who have come through great struggles and trauma. You too will be able to move forward in positive ways, into a brighter, more beautiful future.

Facing the mountain

As you emerge from the broken place which led you inside the covers of this book, the dark valley of despair that you previously trod will one day begin to open out into a whole new landscape of hope and possibility. It might not happen immediately. In fact, it probably won't. But it will be so worth the journey.

Climbing a mountain is hard. Especially if it's the highest mountain you have ever come face to face with. It can seem like an impossibly daunting giant of a task when you first acknowledge the size of it. Setting out with hope and enthusiasm is exhilarating. But there is no guarantee that there won't be hard paths and difficult stumbling blocks along the way. In fact, inevitably there will be. There may be moments when you realise this is so much harder than you thought it was going to be. Sometimes it will take every ounce of effort and resilience that you can muster. But there will also be the knowledge that others have faced similar mountains before you and conquered them successfully. The view from the summit will look like nothing you've ever seen before.

As I write, my son is currently training to trek to Everest Base Camp with his partner. Trekking to a height of 17,598ft over a ten-day climb, acclimatising each day to colder temperatures and increasingly lower levels of oxygen, it will be one of the biggest challenges they have ever undertaken. Through learning how others have faced the journey, they are understanding what is involved. They are getting themselves in the right frame of mind and envisioning the journey, knowing it may be one of the hardest things they have ever done in their lives, but knowing that every step along the way will be worth it. Day after day, week after week, they are training for this, and the steady plod of training will be the foundation for their ultimate success. The training will give them the resilience to stick with the climb even through unexpected setbacks and hard terrain.

Along the way, they may well meet some of the experienced climbers who are going on upwards beyond base camp; those who are attempting to climb even higher, to the very summit of the highest mountain in the world. That's not a climb that anyone can successfully make alone, so those mountaineers will be depending on the expert help of a team of

Sherpas to guide them safely, and they will use mountain yaks to carry their gear.

Doing the training

Experience has taught me that the journey to emotional healing and wellbeing is similar. You need a willingness to understand what is involved and why your mind and body are behaving as they are. Hard journeys require commitment at the outset, and you need to want to engage with what is involved, no matter how hard it feels. Do you want to find a route to a brighter, happier place? Getting your head in the right frame of mind is critical: you must want to want to do it and have the confidence that you can. Others have faced bigger challenges before and have conquered them. So can you. Learning from their experience will help you. Gather your Sherpas and your yaks; you need that support team around you.

When all those things are in place, you can begin. None of the practices in this book are difficult, but neither are they a quick fix. Sometimes the work of healing is slow. You may need to revisit it again and again as different crises hit, because as someone said, 'Life is just one damned thing after another.'[102] Rather like peeling away the layers of an onion, the more you work gently with the pain, the closer you will get to that peaceful place of healing, deep inside yourself. This is not an instant process, but rather a steady, determined climb that requires preparation and training. Consider this little book to be the training manual for your personal ascent out of your pain. That's what it is; a guidebook from someone who has walked a similar path and emerged into a place of peace.

Accepting your situation and practising forgiveness will give you a good foundation for beginning to take things into your own hands and making a new start. Understanding how your body generates its emotional responses, combined with simple techniques to free the tensions from your cells, will enable you to change the dis-ease you experience when you feel yourself heading into emotional free fall without a parachute. When gut-wrenching pain hits, you can learn to express and release your emotions, rather than hitting out in damaging ways, or suppressing the pain and locking it away in your cells.

Understanding that everyone who interacts with you is, like yourself, a work in progress, will help you to take the wider perspective and drop the blame game; a narrative that is only keeping you locked in the pain anyway. Learning how to be tender with your emotions, instead of fighting them, will equip you to ride the ninety-second waves when they surface, recognising that your amazing body is only trying to keep you safe and well.

Spending regular time in prayer will connect you with the deep love at the heart of the universe; the love that can calm every fear and help you through every rocky patch. Practising the methods for settling into stillness, observing your inner world with curiosity and acceptance, and learning to lean on Jesus will be your training for the journey. Like any training, it needs to happen regularly, and it won't always go smoothly. But you need to keep on keeping on. There will be unexpected boulders that trip you up along the way. Sometimes you will stumble and feel as if you are slipping back down. There will be places on the path where you need to stop and get your breath back. And moments when the route no longer seems clear. But in leaning on your support team and returning again and again to the practices in this book, you will be able to pick yourself up and carry on, step by steady step.

Reaping the rewards

I have no doubt that however tough the trek to Everest Base Camp proves to be, standing tall with their boots firmly planted on the slopes of the highest mountain in the world will be an amazing moment for my youngest son and his partner. It will be a most wonderful achievement and will awaken in them the truth that there is no mountain that can't be conquered, and nothing that is impossible. The feeling of achievement will be immense and the view from the roof of the world will be breath-taking. One day this amazing couple will look back on every step and know that it was life-changing and life-enabling.

And so it can be for every step that you take.

Your journey to healing will be no less transformational.

Keep going.

Finally . . .

The principles laid out in this book
can help you to make peace with your painful emotions.

Never forget how deeply you are loved.

The whole resources of God are around you and within you.
God's love is the force enabling you to love yourself
into healing.

Let go of any resistance to that love.

It is a love that forgives everything, a love that can
conquer every fear.

Trust in that truth and tap into that love.

Forgive anyone who has wounded you.
And forgive yourself.
Life is not perfect.
People act out of their own wounds.
Forgive them.

Let go of any negative story in your head.
Replace it with a positive story.

Safely release any strong emotions with symbolic actions.
Let go.

Be aware of the strange sensations in your body.
The physical symptoms are a message that all is not well.

Don't attach a story to them.
Breathe into them.

Hold your Emotions in Awareness and Love.

Accept them and they will dissipate, like a wave on the sea.

Trust in God.
Hand over all your worries into his capable hands.

Take quiet pauses.
Make every thought a prayer.
Be kind to yourself. And to others.
It is the only way to healing and wholeness.

Let the peace of Christ flood you and fill you.

Amen

POSTSCRIPT

Words of Encouragement

Several seasons have been and gone while I have been pondering and working on this book. It has been a while since I first observed the broken, disfigured tree with which I began the opening chapter. The landscape in which it sits overlooks one of my favourite outdoor café spaces.

My gaze always goes to that tree now when I am enjoying a cup of coffee there. I have been fully expecting that the farmer will one day cut it down and it always warms my heart when I find it is still there. I have come to think of it affectionately as 'my' broken tree; the tree which has given me so much inspiration for this writing about brokenness.

Imagine my joy, then, when, on a recent visit I found that things had changed. The broken tree, which to my eyes had looked completely dead two summers before, was sprouting beautiful new green shoots. Something that once seemed impossible had happened. New life had emerged from the tree's damaged past.

And finally, news of that adventure to Everest. My son now has a photograph on his wall of him standing proudly at Everest Base Camp, with the snowy peak of the highest mountain in the world behind him.

Be encouraged. The human spirit can overcome incredibly hard things. And brokenness does not have to have the last word.

New life is possible for you too.

APPENDIX 1

Helpful Resources on Prayer

Digital prayer resources

You will find a wealth of resources online that can help you to explore prayer. Two free resources which I particularly recommend are *Pray As You Go*[103] and *Lectio 365*.[104] Both offer a simple daily reflection and prayer based on Scripture and can act as a helpful springboard into your own prayers.

Taketime[105] has a range of short, guided meditations which can help you to relax, or to explore imaginative prayer.

For a guided online prayer encounter, I recommend you look at the led *Encounter Prayer*[106] sessions of The Christian Healing Mission.

The Bible

If you want to look deeper into the Bible, there are many different translations, all equally good. You can either purchase a paper copy or read the Bible online. For a contemporary version of Scripture, you might consider looking at *The Passion Translation*[107] or The Voice. The free app, YouVersion,[108] gives access to many different Bible translations, plus a whole host of other helpful stuff too.

Whichever version you look at, the chapters of Matthew, Mark, Luke and John are probably the best and the easiest ones to read first. In that section of the Bible, you will find many of the accounts of Jesus' life.

Healing stories and imaginative prayer

The following accounts of Jesus healing people are good passages to immerse yourself in through imaginative prayer:

Mark 10:46-52:	Jesus asks, 'What do you want me to do for you?' and then does it.
John 8:1-11:	Jesus forgives someone who has broken the law.
John 5:1-9:	Jesus asks, 'Would you like to get well?' and then enables it.
Mark 2:1-12:	Jesus shows that forgiveness is part of healing.
John 9:1-41:	Jesus heals a man who was born blind.
Mark 5:21-34:	Jesus heals someone who risks reaching out to him for healing.
Luke 8:22-25:	Jesus calms a terrifying storm.

Friendship with others who pray

You may find it very helpful to join up with others who pray. Prayer is often more powerful when two or more people pray together, and friendship with others who pray will give you both confidence and support.

If you don't know anyone who prays, why not just walk into a church one day? If you can find one where you feel at home, that will be a good starting point from which to build relationships with other people who pray. There are as many different styles of church as there are people; some very traditional, others more relaxed and informal. Try out a few until you find the one that's right for you.

Retreat houses

There are many retreat houses[109] around the country where you will find safe space, a warm welcome, and people who will listen to your story and pray with you. These spaces are usually open to people of any faith or none, and they are ideal environments in which to rest and regroup and to experience the love of Jesus in a tangible way. Just stepping out of everyday life for a few days, with no specific agenda, can be enormously helpful in finding a measure of peace in an otherwise stressful life. You can visit for a short stay as an individual guest or join one of their many different courses. Most of them have bursary funds to offer financial help towards the cost of your stay if you need that.

APPENDIX 2

Further Healing Resources Written by Pat Marsh

Pathways to Healing CD series

CDs to help you to encounter Jesus through immersive experiences with the healing scriptures.

The CDs feature Scripture, music, sound effects and guided meditation with the healing stories.

CD1: *Take Up Your Mat*[110]
CD2: *Calming the Storm*[111]

Dwelling in the Psalms book

Contemporary interpretations and prayers for each of the psalms, drawing out what each psalm teaches about healing.[112]

All the above are available from Christian bookshops and conventional online sources or directly from Pat at www.patmarsh.co.uk

Healing retreats

Pat leads healing retreats at various places. Details can be found on her website (as above).

APPENDIX 3

Sources of Help in an Emergency

If you feel that your life is in danger:

Don't hesitate. Call 999.

Nothing is more important than your safety and you will be treated with consideration and respect.

If you need urgent help with your mental health, at any time of the day or night:

Call 111 and press 2

This will connect you to a mental health professional who can offer immediate support and guidance.

If you just need to talk, at any time of the day or night:

For free in-the-moment confidential support to talk about anything that is troubling you, no matter how difficult:

Call 116 123 to talk to *Samaritans*
or
text *'SHOUT'* to *85258* to contact the *Shout Crisis Text Line*

If you are already working with a GP, counsellor, or therapist:

Discuss your situation with them and seek their help.

About the Author

When you first see someone healed by prayer, it changes every concept you ever had of God. This happened for Pat when a chronically disabled lady started dancing around a room during a guided scriptural meditation that Pat was leading. Since that moment, nearly twenty years ago, Pat's heart for guiding others to healing through encounters with Jesus has grown exponentially. Today she works primarily as an award-winning writer, retreat leader and prayerful listener.

She writes scripturally based meditations which enable people to place themselves at the heart of the Gospel stories and encounter Jesus. These meditations are a key part of her retreats. Some of them are recorded on CD in her *Pathways to Healing* series: *Take Up Your Mat* and *Calming the Storm.* At the height of the pandemic, she created an online series, *Prayerful Moments in the Pandemic.*[113]

Dwelling in the Psalms, written by Pat, draws out the healing lessons of the psalms, comprising a contemporary interpretation, a devotional thought and a prayer for each of the 150 psalms. This latest book,

Healing Life's Wounds, is her latest resource for helping people to heal.

Pat has also published three collections of poetry: *Whispers of Love*,[114] *Silent Strength*[115] and *The Gift of a Cross*.[116] She blogs and uploads some of her writing at www.patmarsh.co.uk and she can also be found on Facebook.

When she is not writing or leading retreats, Pat can often be found drinking good coffee by the side of a lake and photographing the birds. On a sunny day, she can never resist buying an ice cream.

Acknowledgements

This book would not have come into being without the support of many people. To all of them I owe a debt of gratitude. I offer my heartfelt thanks to the following:

Jesus, without whose love in my life none of this would ever have happened.

Irene Nicholls, for her deep prayerful friendship and her openness to God, which initiated and guided the birth of this book.

Joanna Legg-Bagg, Nicci Gagel and all the team at Penhurst Retreat Centre who blessed me with prayerful friendship, amazing hospitality and supportive space in which to complete several stages of the writing.

The Coverdale Trust and my ministry sponsors for their much-valued financial support.

Tony Collins for his wisdom and advice.

Malcolm Down, Sarah Grace and their team for bringing this book to publication.

Sheila Jacobs for her wise, patient and perceptive editorial advice.

Jan McFarlane, Margaret Silf, Gilana Young, Catriona Futter, Geraldine Elliot-Smith, John Ryeland, Penelope Swithinbank, Tony & Jilly Horsfall, Emily Owen, Amy Boucher Pye, Susan Alexander Yates, Vicki Cottingham, Sheila Jacobs and Edwina Gateley for their generosity in taking time to read and endorse the final version of the book.

Chris Duffett, Suzanne Owen, Penny Button, Barbara Dodd, Irene Nicholls and Gill Hancock for kindly reading and giving important feedback on early drafts of the book.

The countless people whom I have met and ministered to in retreat houses over the years. From all of them I have probably learned far more about healing than I have ever imparted.

The many and varied practitioners of Christian healing, from whom I continue to learn, with special thanks to John Ryeland of The Christian Healing Mission and Wes Sutton of the Acorn Christian Healing Foundation.

Those professionals who have skilfully helped me through my own healing journey, with specific thanks to Tricia Hall-Matthews, Jane Besly and Karen Collins.

Angela Rogerson for her discerning and supportive spiritual direction.

Acknowledgements

Chris Finn for his teachings about how the mind works.

My son Dave for his thoughts on dealing with anxieties.

Last, but certainly not least, my dear friends, Di Saxton, Penny Sherrington, Penny Button, Barbara Dodd, Maggie Jeays and Jill Hoffmann who all faithfully prayed me through the long and winding writing process. I couldn't have done this without you.

Finally, I give thanks for all the struggles and the joys, the difficulties and the wonder of the life that I have led – even, with hindsight, the tough bits. Every day has shaped the writing of this book, and I am thankful for it all.

End Notes

Chapter 1: Feeling Broken

[1] Brené Brown, PhD, MSW, https://brenebrown.com/art/dare-to-lead-when-we-have-the-courage-to-walk-into-our-story-and-own-it/ (accessed 13.2.25).

[2] Wayne G. Trotman, *London: Metropolis of the Future* film review, www.redmoon.vo.uk (accessed 22.4.24).

[3] Jo Saxton, *The Dream of You* (Oxford: Monarch Books, New edition, 2018), p. 10.

[4] Simon Parke, https://simonparke.com/therapy/my-approach-to-mental-health (accessed 26.1.25).

[5] Brené Brown, PhD, MSW, https://brenebrown.com/art/dare-to-lead-when-we-have-the-courage-to-walk-into-our-story-and-own-it/ (accessed 13.2.25).

[6] C.S. Lewis, *The Lion, the Witch and the Wardrobe* (London: HarperCollins, 2009.)

[7] Marléne R. Shaw, https://marleneroseshaw.com/out-of-fear-into-love-book/ (accessed 12.02.25)

[8] Patrick Regan, *Honesty Over Silence* (Surrey: CWR, 2018), Kindle loc. 827.

[9] Regan, *Honesty Over Silence*, Kindle loc. 1092.

Chapter 2: Getting Started

[10] Anne Lamott, *Bird by Bird* (Edinburgh: Canongate Canons, 2020).

[11] Matthew 6:34; Matthew 10:31; Psalm 145:8; Luke 6:37; Matthew 11:28; Psalm 106:1; Psalm 46:10, Mark 6:31; Matthew 6:6.

[12] John 5:1-9.

[13] Mark 10:46-52.

[14] John 5:6.

[15] Mark 10:51.

[16] Victoria Priya, 'Has Your Wound Become an Addiction?', https://unveilingtiamat.com/has-your-wound-become-an-addiction/ (accessed 26.1.25).

[17] Brené Brown, PhD, MSW, 'Own Our History. Change the Story', https://brenebrown.com/articles/2015/06/18/own-our-history-change-the-story/ (accessed 26.1.25).

[18] Matthew 28:20.

[19] Matthew 11:28.

[20] Anne D. LeClaire, *Listening Below the Noise* (New York: Harper, 2009), p. 146.

[21] Some content taken from *Dare to Journey with Henri Nouwen* by Charles Ringma. Copyright © (2000). Used by permission of NavPress, represented by Tyndale House Publishers, a division of Tyndale House Ministries. All rights reserved.

[22] Frank Skinner, *A Comedian's Prayer Book* (London: Hodder & Stoughton, 2021), p. 9.

[23] Psalm 104:24-30, *MSG*.

[24] Psalm 139:14, NIV.

Chapter 3: Those Strange Sensations

[25] Simon Parke, *The Journey Home* (London: Bloomsbury Paperbacks, 2011), p. 166.

[26] Barbara Brown Taylor, *Learning to Walk in the Dark* (Norwich: Canterbury Press, 2014), Kindle loc. 85.

[27] https://steer.education (accessed 12.2.25).

[28] Simon P. Walker, *The Undefended Life* (Great Britain: Human Ecology Partners, 2013), Kindle loc. 81.

29 Katie A. Ports, et al., 'Adverse Childhood Experiences and the Presence of Cancer Risk Factors in Adulthood', *Journal of Pediatric Nursing*, vol. 44, 2019, pp. 81-96.

30 Team GB, *Super Saturday,* https://m.youtube.com/watch?v=gZsdbNFb6H8 (accessed 4.3.23).

31 1 John 4.18.

32 Mark 5:36.

Chapter 4: Defusing Your Emotions

33 Miriam Greenspan, *Healing through the Dark Emotions* (Boulder, CO: Shambhala Publications Inc, 2004), Kindle loc. 3875.

34 Niki Hardy, *Breathe Again* (Grand Rapids, MI: Revell, 2019), p. 130.

35 Sam Harris, *Waking Up* (Cambridge: Black Swan, 2015), p. 28.

36 Greenspan, *Healing through the Dark Emotions,* Kindle loc. 1008.

37 Gail Brenner, 'The Highly Intelligent Approach to Difficult Emotions', https://gailbrenner.com (accessed 13.12.21).

38 David Kessler and Elisabeth Kübler-Ross, *Life Lessons* (London: Simon & Schuster UK, 2014), quoted in 'When You Don't Choose Love You Choose Fear', awakin.org/v2/read/view.php?tid=680 (accessed 26.1.25).

39 Dr Joan Rosenberg, 'Emotional Mastery: The Gifted Wisdom of Unpleasant Feelings', [Video], TED conferences, September 2016, https://m.youtube.com/watch?v=EKy19WzkPxE (accessed 22.4.24).

Chapter 5: The Inner Story

40 Cynthia Curry, 'Is this you?', https://cynthiacurry.uk/is-this-you/ (accessed 26.1.25).

41 Attributed to the Dalai Lama and others, www.goodreads.com/quotes/9666529-pain-is-inevitable-suffering-is-optional (accessed 11.2.25).

[42] Greenspan, *Healing through the Dark Emotions*, Kindle loc. 1697.

[43] 'Soulful Vision', soulfulvision.uk (accessed 26.1.25).

Chapter 6: New Perspectives

[44] Allison Aars, quoted in *The Minds Journal*, https://themindsjournal.com/quotes/when-you-finally-learn-that-a persons-behaviour-has-more/ (accessed 26.1.25).

[45] Attributed to Abraham Lincoln, but may have originated with Alphonse Karr, www.goodreads.com/quotes/10564364-we-can-complain-because-rose-bushes-have-thorns-or-rejoice (accessed 11.2.25).

[46] Cathy Madavan, *Irrepressible* (London: SPCK, 2020), p. 60.

[47] Weizmann Institute of Science, 'Quantum Theory Demonstrated: Observation Affects Reality' (ScienceDaily, 27 February 1998), www.sciencedaily.com/releases/1998/02/980227055013.htm (accessed 26.01.25).

[48] Dietrich Bonhoeffer, *Letters and Papers from Prison* (London: SCM Press, 1953).

Chapter 7: The Question of Forgiveness

[49] Archbishop Desmond Tutu and Rev Mpho Tutu, *The Book of Forgiving* (New York: Harper Collins, 2015), p. 137.

[50] Russ Parker, *Forgiveness is Healing* (London: SPCK, 2011).

[51] Matthew 6:9-13.

[52] Sue Atkinson, *Struggling to Forgive: Moving on from Trauma* (Oxford: Monarch, 2014), p. 56.

[53] Nelson Mandela, *Long Walk to Freedom* (London: Abacus, 1995).

[54] See Luke 4:18.

[55] Matthew 26:28, CEV.

[56] Mark 2:1-5, NIV.

[57] John 8:1-11.

End Notes

58 Atkinson, *Struggling to Forgive*, p. 135.

59 Karen L. Swartz, 'Forgiveness: Your Health Depends On It', www.hopkinsmedicine.org/health/wellness-and-prevention/forgiveness-your-health-depends-on-it (accessed 26.1.25).

60 Tutu and Tutu, *The Book of Forgiving*, p. 3.

61 See Luke 4:18.

62 'Agape World', https://www.agapeworldreconciliation.org (accessed 26.1.25).

63 Some content taken from *Dare to Journey with Henri Nouwen* by Charles Ringma. Copyright © (2000). Used by permission of NavPress, represented by Tyndale House Publishers, a division of Tyndale House Ministries. All rights reserved.

Chapter 8: Letting Go

64 Nathan Peterson, 'Finding Freedom, and Ourselves, in Letting Go', https://nathanpeterson.net/finding-freedom-and-ourselves-in-letting-go/ (accessed 26.1.25).

65 Henri Nouwen, *The Road to Daybreak* (London: Darton, Longman & Todd, 2013), p. 81.

Chapter 9: Actively Forgiving

66 Tutu and Tutu, *The Book of Forgiving*, p. 5.

67 'Versions of the Lord's Prayer', https://cofewinchester.contentfiles.net/media/assets/file/Versions-of-The-Lords-Prayer.pdf (accessed 22.4.24).

68 Matthew 18:22.

Chapter 10: The Problem of Worry

69 Julian of Norwich, *Showings* (Mahwah, NJ: Paulist Press, 1978).

70 Matthew 18:21-22.

71 See Luke 4:18.

[72] Matthew 6:34.

[73] 1 John 4:8.

[74] David G. Benner, *Surrender to Love* (Downers Grove, IL: InterVarsity Press, 2015), p. 20.

[75] Attributed to Mother Teresa, www.goodreads.com/quotes/1246-the-hunger-for-love-is-much-more-difficult-to-remove (accessed 11.2.25).

[76] Luke 15:11-31.

[77] Romans 8:39, CEV.

[78] www.charliemackesy.com/sculptures (accessed 26.1.25).

[79] shop.charliemackesy.com/products/prodigal-son (accessed 26.1.25).

[80] Jeremiah 29:11.

[81] Isaiah 41:10 .

[82] 1 Peter 5:7.

[83] Attributed to Mark Twain, www.goodreads.com/quotes/201777-i-ve-had-a-lot-of-worries-in-my-life-most (11.2.25).

Chapter 11: The Power of the Pause

[84] Tim Stead, *Mindfulness and Christian Spirituality* (London: SPCK, 2016), p. 100.

[85] Exodus 15:26.

[86] Stephen Cottrell, *Do Nothing to Change Your Life* (London: Church House Publishing, 2020).

[87] Sharon Garlough Brown, in Foreword to Amy Boucher Pye, *7 Ways to Pray* (London: SPCK Publishing, 2021).

[88] Attributed to Alexis Carrel, www.azquotes.com/quote/836118 (accessed 13.2.25).

[89] Attributed to Alexis Carrel, www.powerquotations.com/quote/the-influence-of-prayer-on (accessed 13.2.25).

[90] 1 Thessalonians 5:17.

[91] https://acornchristian.org (accessed 12.2.25).

[92] Russ Parker, *In Search of Wholeness course* (Nottingham: St John's Extension Studies, 2000), Unit 6:82.

[93] Psalm 46:10.

[94] Isaiah 30:15, NIV.

[95] Romans 8:28.

[96] Matthew 14:13, Matthew 14:23, Mark 1:35, Mark 6:46, Luke 4:42, Luke 5:16.

[97] John 14:27.

Chapter 12: One Step at a Time

[98] Attributed to Lao Tzu, www.brainyquote.com/quotes/lao_tzu_137141 (accessed 26.1.25).

[99] https://kintsugihope.com (accessed 26.1.25).

[100] Regan, *Honesty Over Silence*, Kindle loc. 388.

[101] Sheridan Voysey, *Resurrection Year* (Nashville, TN: Thomas Nelson, US, 2013), p. xii.

[102] Attributed here to Elbert Hubbard but also attributed to others, www.brainyquote.com/quotes/elbert_hubbard_124954 (accessed 22.4.24).

Appendix 1: Helpful Resources on Prayer

[103] https://pray-as-you-go.org/home (accessed (26.1.25).

[104] www.24-7prayer.com (accessed 26.1.25).

[105] https://taketime.org.uk (accessed 26.1.25).

[106] www.encounterprayer.net (accessed 26.1.25).

[107] Brian Simmons, *The Passion Translation* (BroadStreet Publishing, MN: Savage, 2011).

[108] www.youversion.com/the-bible-app/ (accessed 26.1.25).

[109] You can find more information about the variety of retreat houses at www.retreats.org.uk (accessed 26.1.25).

Appendix 2: Further Healing Resources Written by Pat Marsh

[110] Pat Marsh, *Take Up Your Mat* (CD) (Truro: Pat Marsh, 2016).

[111] Pat Marsh, *Calming the Storm* (CD) (Truro: Pat Marsh, 2016).

[112] Pat Marsh, *Dwelling in the Psalms* (Stowmarket: Kevin Mayhew, 2019).

About the Author

[113] https://prayerfulmoments.blogspot.com (accessed 17.2.25).

[114] Pat Marsh, *Whispers of Love* (West Horsley: Onwards and Upwards Publications, 2011).

[115] Pat Marsh, *Silent Strength* (Peterborough: Methodist Publishing House, 2005).

[116] Pat Marsh, *The Gift of a Cross* (Peterborough: Methodist Publishing House, 2006).

www.ingramcontent.com/pod-product-compliance
Lightning Source LLC
Chambersburg PA
CBHW060530100426
42743CB00009B/1482